MY INCREDIBLE
WORLD
CUP
JOURNEY

AROUND THE GLOBE
FROM ARGENTINA TO BRAZIL

MY INCREDIBLE

WORLD CUP JOURNEY

AROUND THE GLOBE
FROM ARGENTINA TO BRAZIL

MICHAEL RENOUF

FAIRPLAY
PUBLISHING

First published in 2022 by Fair Play Publishing
PO Box 4101, Balgowlah Heights, NSW 2093, Australia

www.fairplaypublishing.com.au

ISBN: 978-1-925914-31-3
ISBN: 978-1-925914-32-0 (ePub)

© Michael Renouf 2022
The moral rights of the author have been asserted.

Cover design and typesetting by Lisa Rafferty

All inquiries should be made to the Publisher via
sales@fairplaypublishing.com.au

NATIONAL
LIBRARY
OF AUSTRALIA

A catalogue record of this book is available from the
National Library of Australia.

CONTENTS

Prologue

1   Argentina 1978

25   Spain 1982

46   Mexico 1986

63   Italy 1990

80   USA 1994

92   France 1998

108   Japan and South Korea 2002

124   Germany 2006

140   South Africa 2010

154   Brazil 2014

173   Epilogue

175   About The Author

PROLOGUE

I did not grow up in a football-mad household. My dad had much preferred boxing and even on occasion the Saturday afternoon wrestling if Big Daddy was on, whom he had once given a lift to a show when the grappler's car broke down.

All the same I loved the game from the moment I kicked a ball in our back garden.

And now it was here, my first World Cup televised live all the way from Argentina and featuring sixteen nations from around the globe. Countries such as Brazil, the Netherlands, West Germany and Scotland would enthral an eleven-year-old boy and so it would be, every four years for ever more.

I, like so many others, have been captivated by images of great goals, dastardly deeds, moments of genius, outright cheating and much more from five continents in five different decades and with any luck, there will be so much more to come. It has given me more heartbreak than pleasure, but I keep coming back for more and whatever happens, I know I always will.

Although only won by eight countries in its almost ninety-year history, the World Cup is cherished around the globe on a level no other event can hope to match. This is my experience of the greatest show on earth.

ARGENTINA 1978

The World Cup Virgin

Like every little boy or girl who loves football, your first World Cup is similar to your first kiss. However, unlike your first kiss, it is rarely bettered, unless you have the opportunity to see your country hoist the trophy skywards or go to a finals. So far, I have had the opportunity to do only one of these while eternally hoping for the other.

My first World Cup was shortly after my eleventh birthday and was broadcast around the world from the distant and exotic shores of Argentina. It was a far cry from the provincial county of Wiltshire in England and infinitely more exotic than the local sport of tractor pulling!

In the days when live football on television was a rarity, the prospect of thirty-eight games played over three and a half weeks filled me with excitement, the likes of which I had never experienced before. In fact, the only live games I can recall watching before that time of any sort were three FA Cup finals, in 1976, 1977 and 1978, along with a game that gave me my first real World Cup memory.

I support Manchester United, so the game to which I lost my virginity ended in disappointment. Sound familiar? As my team went down 1–0 to second division Southampton, my 'friend' across the road, a Liverpool fan, as most schoolchildren in England were in those days, called our house phone right on the final whistle. This was many years before everybody started walking around with mobile phones glued to their ears, and he shouted 1–0 down the phone in his prepubescent voice, before hanging up firmly. Thanks to the proximity of my school to the city of Southampton, less than forty-five minutes' drive, the other popular team at my school were the Saints. You can imagine what Monday morning brought, back at school after a controversial match. No amount of arguing that Bobby Stokes' late winner was offside would change the result, as snooty-nosed little runts accompanied by teachers tore into me and another two United

1

supporters. It was sweet revenge a year later when United beat Liverpool 2–1 with a goal that deflected off Jimmy Greenhoff's chest, past Ray Clemence and into the Liverpool goal. No prizes for guessing what I did as the referee brought a halt to proceedings that afternoon.

We tuned into ITV on November 16, 1977, as England beat Italy 2–0 at Wembley, thanks to goals from Kevin Keegan and Trevor Brooking, a victory that sent them top of the group by two points. With both teams possessing the same goal difference, all English hopes rested on Italy slipping up in their last game of the campaign which would be played in Rome. Unfortunately, for anybody with an allegiance to the Three Lions, the visitors to the Italian capital would be Luxembourg, one of the whipping boys of European football. Of course, the twice previous champions were not going to let such an opportunity slip and I woke to a cloudy December morning the day after the game to discover that Italy had strolled to a 3–0 victory. For the first time since 1970, England would not be playing in the World Cup finals.

But there would be British representation in South America the following year, after Scotland had topped a three-team group containing European champions Czechoslovakia and near neighbour Wales. The 'Celtic Derby' that saw the Scotland squad advance and then head into the recording studio to record their official World Cup song with none other than Rod Stewart was mired in controversy.

Wales' 'home game' was being played at Anfield for a variety of reasons, including money. It was a decision that backfired. Scottish fans travelled down to Liverpool in their thousands, as it was much closer for them than Cardiff. With less than quarter of an hour left and the fate of the Celtic cousins finely balanced, the packed stadium witnessed Scotland's Joe Jordan rise with Welsh defender David Jones to contest Asa Hartford's throw in from the left into the Welsh penalty area. A hand punched the ball, which the referee spotted, before awarding a spot-kick, which Don Masson slotted past Dai Davies to put Scotland in front. Where was the controversy? Well, Jordan had done a 'Maradona' nine years before the Argentinian deceived a Tunisian referee at the 1986 World Cup with his 'Hand of God' goal. The terrifyingly positive Ally MacLeod, who could make major heart surgery sound like a relaxing trip to an upmarket spa, was Scotland's manager and pied piper-like would lead Ally's army on their merry way across the Atlantic Ocean.

The 1978 Cup final came and went in a blur as Ipswich Town, under the stewardship of Bobby Robson, who would later take charge of England at the '86 and '90 finals, upset the mighty Arsenal. Perhaps MacLeod was right and a small nation like Scotland could be crowned world champions. He was everywhere you looked, as sponsors in Scotland entered an emerging market, jumping at the chance to be associated with a team that was going to win the whole thing. Add to this the undeniably catchy Ally's Tartan Army by Scottish comedian Andy Cameron (who like Stewart was actually born in England) that reached the top ten and was even performed on *Top of the Pops*, I, along with thousands of others, had fallen for a big con for the first time in my life, believing that I would be watching Scotland all the way to the final. Companies such as Chrysler with their highly paid directors and marketing departments should have carried out far better due diligence; I, on the other hand, was eleven years old.

The draw, which paired Scotland with Peru, Iran and the Netherlands, was held in Buenos Aires in January 1978. A three-year-old boy called Ricardo, the grandson of FIFA President Dr Joao Havelange, totally unaware of the fate he would be bestowing on the teams involved, helped in the process of constructing the draw. While the Dutch would be a tough test, many in the Scottish team believed they would breeze past the other two and with first and second in the group qualifying for the next round, felt they were pretty much guaranteed to get through.

Determined not to miss an opportunity, on May 25 the Scottish FA held a going-away party at Hampden Park, in effect an open-top bus parade before the tournament. How could that possibly backfire? Well, over the next month, in more ways than even the most dour, grumpy and pessimistic Scot could imagine. The players and manager had to walk out individually to the acclaim of the crowd and even MacLeod had the good grace to look embarrassed. If you were prepared to part with thirty pence—the Scots were not going to be outdone by the Welsh FA when it came to filling their coffers—you could buy a programme. Featured on the cover were Córdoba and Mendoza, the cities where Scotland would contest its group games, along with Buenos Aires where they would play their second-round games, providing they made it that far. That would occur if Scotland finished second in their section, so at least somebody had a sense of realism, as they had been drawn in a group that contained the 1974 runners-up. Or did somebody in the marketing department have loftier expectations, as this was also the venue for the final? I would love to know.

World Cup fever captured the British Isles in all its technicolour glory. We all have stories of what we sacrificed or had to do to watch a game, often exaggerated, but I wager none took as much effort as the following. In the remote Highlands of Scotland, a small village on the Knoydart Peninsula had no television signal, but the locals were not going to allow this small matter to deter them from following the team's progress in Argentina. The answer was simple. Over four weekends, they sweated and swore, swilled and swung as they dug and dug for four miles in all, so they could lay a cable to an aerial at the top of a neighbouring mountain. The last guests at the party had arrived.

On their Powerage tour, Aussie rock gods AC/DC, formed by brothers Malcolm and Angus Young, performed at the Glasgow Apollo in Scottish football jerseys. This was no idle jumping on the bandwagon; the brothers were born in the city before moving with their families to Australia as part of the Assisted Passage Migration Scheme, or to use the colloquial term, 'Ten Pound Poms'.

The Royal Mail, not prepared to be outdone by diggers or rockers, spades or guitars, designed and printed two stamps, an 11p first class and a 9p second class, showing the Scottish players celebrating winning the World Cup. This is not something done on speculation every time a British team gets to the finals, but more proof of how ludicrous the hype was surrounding this group of players. For some reason they were never circulated!

The Beginning

The tournament would be disputed by sixteen of the best teams in the world. Missing for the first time since 1958 were Bulgaria and Uruguay but with teams such as Brazil, Argentina, West Germany, Netherlands, Italy and Hungary, a feast of football awaited my eager young eyes.

On the first day of June, I settled down, Panini sticker book in hand, to watch my first World Cup match. It would be reigning champions

West Germany facing off against neighbours, rivals and the team that finished third on German soil four years earlier, Poland. The Poles saw it as a chance for revenge and their manager, Jan Gmoch, even declared this team was better than the one from four years earlier, who after five straight victories in that tournament, including triumphs over Argentina and Italy, had gone down 1–0 to tonight's opponents. Had Poland won that game it would have meant an appearance in the final. The comment was just not bravado, as within their ranks was Grzegorz Lato who had finished top scorer with seven goals at the previous World Cup. They also had several other survivors from '74 who had picked up a host of individual awards and accolades that year. Wladyslaw Zmuda (Best Young Player) and Andrzej Szarmach (Silver Shoe) were both at the World Cup, and Kazimierz Deyna, who had finished third in the Ballon d'Or. They had also added Zbigniew Boniek, who would go on to be one of the greatest Polish players of all time. Between the sticks they had the vastly experienced Jan Tomaszewski, who Brian Clough had famously labelled a clown on the notorious night when his performance prevented England reaching the finals in West Germany. This was the second tournament in a row where Poland would be strutting their stuff on the world stage while England sat at home nursing broken dreams. Who was laughing now?

The scene was set for a pulsating start but as this beautiful game of ours does at the most inopportune moments, it served up a 0–0 draw, the fourth World Cup finals in a row that the opening game ended scoreless. I would have to wait to see my first World Cup finals goal. Luckily, the next day the tournament had three games scheduled. Tunisia faced Mexico in a match that was not shown live on television in the UK. The game in which the North Africans ran out 3–1 winners was significant, as it was the first time an African team had won a game at the finals. However, ITV was showing France taking on Italy and the French wasted little time getting into the swing of things with Bernard Lacombe finding the back of the Italian net after only thirty-seven seconds, with a fine header after a magnificent sweeping counter attack. It was the eighth-fastest goal in World Cup history to that point in time. The tournament was now alive. I had witnessed my first World Cup goal, scored fittingly by the nation that had scored the first ever goal of any type in the tournament's history, when France defeated Mexico 4–1 on the opening day of the 1930 finals in Uruguay.

Argentina and Hungary were the other two combatants in Group 1, labelled as the group of death. This is normally just a footballing euphemism but with Argentina under the oppressive regime of the military junta, the description on this occasion had a far more sinister ring to it. They would face off at 11:00 p.m. UK time, far too late for me to be allowed to watch. I had negotiated permission prior to the tournament to be able to watch all of Scotland's games plus the final, along with Brazil's games if they were on early enough and 'selected other games', at my parents' discretion. I certainly was not going to be allowed to dictate the television schedule in a house with only one television and twenty-five days of football ahead. Luckily, there were only three channels to choose from so not too much competition from 'what's on the other side'. Also, there would often be two or three days between games which I am sure helped my cause to consume as much live football as possible.

Argentina, being the hosts, had arranged that their first-round games would be played after their opponents, hence they always knew the lie of the land. Part of this was genuine so the home audience could watch their team in the evening, but it was just one of many things that went in the hosts' favour, some darker than others.

Something many Argentinians felt was not in their favour was the omission of a seventeen-year-old wonder kid who went by the name of Diego Armando Maradona. He had made the original twenty-five man 'concetracion' but was cut along with Humberto Bravo and Lito Bottaniz when the squad was reduced to the twenty-two who would be representing their country at the finals. Maradona, who admitted to crying buckets over this decision, never forgave manager Cesar Menotti, although he did develop a respect for El Flaco, the skinny one, for the wisdom he shared with him throughout his career.

The Hungarian manager, Lajos Baróti, declared, "Everything, even the air is in favour of Argentina." The Eastern European side took an early lead before Leopoldo Luque, who looked every bit a typical Argentinian gaucho, with his flowing locks and a moustache of which Magnum PI, Tom Selleck, would be proud, equalised with less than ten minutes of the game remaining. The winning goal was firstly credited to Norberto

Alonso wearing number 1 by Argentinian TV, but good old John Motson commentating for the British television audience was not so easily fooled. He correctly credited Daniel Bertoni. No, that is not a mistake on my part; they were not crediting the strike to the goalkeeper, just the wrong substitute, as Argentina had assigned their squad numbers alphabetically. The goal was not the final drama of the night as two of the Hungarian team received their marching orders shortly before the final whistle. That was some achievement, as the only other sending-off in the entire tournament would be the Netherlands Dick Nanninga.

June 3 was the third day in a run of games being played that would give me memories that are still vividly fresh today. It would be my first 'double header'. To begin with, I was going to watch everyone's second team, Brazil, beat Sweden and then sit back and witness Scotland walking through Peru. However, a Welshman along with several Peruvians had other ideas.

Clive Thomas and That Disallowed Goal

At the previous World Cup, Brazil had metamorphosed from the brilliant, beautiful, ball-caressing team that ruled the world in 1970 to a more workman-like and brutal side. It was against this backdrop that the Scandinavian's manager, Georg Ericson, had called them "dirty" and praised the appointment of Clive Thomas who he described as "a strong referee ... generally regarded as the best one here".

Just as we were finishing the appetiser, we were then treated to an astonishing sight. Brazil had been awarded a corner and the linesman had noticed the ball was not positioned correctly in the quadrant so made Brazilian substitute Nelinho reposition it, before he sent over a perfect cross as the clock ticked by ninety minutes plus seven and then eight seconds of injury time. Zico got his header on target, sending the ball into the back of the Swedish net just as the referee whistled for full-time. The pedantic pea blower disallowed the goal in a way even VAR has never managed. Imagine Thomas in charge of a game now. Cristiano Ronaldo would have a goal disallowed for being too Portuguese whilst Zlatan Ibrahimovic would have at least one strike ruled out because of his haircut. The Welsh whistler, although I guess in Brazil they may have a different name for him, deemed Zico's effort just a fraction of a second too late. Thomas walked off the pitch crossing his arms like a manic water diviner, albeit minus his divining rods, with the bemused Brazilian team trailing in his wake, possibly too dumbfounded to raise any real protest.

At the time, I thought he was right to disallow the Selecao's goal but as I have got older I have realised the world is not black and white, as those with a cause to preach would have you believe, but in reality many shades of grey. I now look upon this as a really bad decision and not in the spirit of the game. How could any referee be that accurate? Although Thomas himself does not see it that way, stating that "Zico was too late, possibly only four-tenths of a second too late, but too late nevertheless". The next morning, after a night of alleged nightclubbing with ex-Welsh rugby union star Cliff Morgan and then head of BBC Sport and commentator David Coleman, Thomas's dream of following in fellow Brit Jack Taylor's footsteps, who had refereed the 1974 final, was over. He was awoken by a member of FIFA's referee committee, Friedrich Seipelt, and given the news that he was to be sent home. He would never again be invited to dine at FIFA's main restaurant.

We will never know if Ericson's praising of Thomas affected the ego of a man that never shied away from the limelight. What we do know is, the referee known as 'The Book', for being a stickler for the rules, had refused to sign a contract FIFA had sent out before the finals, that stipulated that the men in the middle should not talk to the press. Whatever happened, he would have his say.

Never mind, that was only my second team, now it was on to the evening's main entertainment for which I would be joined upstairs by my mum and dad. Years before, my parents had bought a petrol station with workshops and a bungalow attached and Dad had added an upstairs to the living accommodation which subsequently became our lounge. Thanks to some miscalculations the steps were huge, so the risk of injury was nearly as high watching a game as actually playing in one.

The Tartan Army

There was a large travelling contingent of Scottish fans who had made their way across the water, any way they could, to cheer on their heroes. This was long before the proliferation of transatlantic flights that are available today. One fan's dad worked as security at a dock in northern Scotland and found out a grain boat was in harbour about to go to Argentina. His dad rang him and suggested he "get down here now", which he subsequently did. Four hours later, the pair found themselves working their passage across the Atlantic. Others raised money however they could for the expedition, selling prized possessions such as motorbikes, cars or in one extreme case, a Glasgow butcher sold his shop.

When the Scottish team had left Hampden Park's premature celebration, they did so in front of thirty thousand people and were welcomed by the same number in the town of Alta Gracia near Cordoba. Despite the warm welcome, the first act of Scotland's impending disaster was about to unfold, as the coach broke down and some of the players were required to get out and push. Can you imagine the reaction from most of today's players if they were asked to do the same? They then checked into their hotel and things did not get any better. The rooms were still being prepared, with carpets being laid, beds without mattresses and a waterless swimming pool. Well, at least the Club Atlético Sportivo training pitch would be decent. Think again: after some ankle injuries on the overgrown, uneven surface, the Scots soon changed to a better facility in Cordoba, but this resulted in having to endure an hour-long journey each way on the rickety bus. Add to this, and not for the first or last time in World Cup history, a row about player bonuses and rumours of players drinking until the wee hours and you could see the Scottish dream starting to unravel.

Now all I knew about Peru before the game was that it was the original home of my favourite children's character Paddington Bear and thanks to my sticker album, that they had a snazzy kit. Ninety minutes later, it appeared that with those small nuggets of information, I knew more than the entire Scottish squad and back-room staff about their opponents. The game began as everyone in Britain expected with Scotland taking the lead within fifteen minutes, thanks to a Joe Jordan goal. The forward who lost his two front teeth during a Leeds United reserve match wore dentures off the pitch but would cannily remove them prior to games and present an image to his opponents of somebody you would not want to mess with at closing time in the East End of Glasgow. He had become one of my favourite players thanks to his recent transfer to Manchester United. It was just before half-time when the first semblance of reality hit Scotland and Los Incas equalised. Still, forty-five minutes to put things right for the future world champions and in the sixty-fourth minute Don Masson had the chance from the penalty spot after skipper Bruce Ricoh was taken out in the 18-yard box. Unfortunately, it was not the greatest of spot-kicks and Ramon Quiroga turned it around the post for nothing more than a corner.

For many, the Derby County pair should not have been on the pitch, preferring Archie Gemmill and Graeme Souness, especially based on their performances leading up to the finals. However, by the seventy-fifth minute the faith MacLeod had shown in the men that got his team to Argentina had started to wane and he would replace them with Gemmill and Lou Macari. In between the penalty miss and substitutions, Peru had taken the lead thanks to a magnificent strike from outside the box by Teófilo Cubillas, who celebrated arms aloft, a cross between an Inca emperor and Muhammad Ali on fight night, and was rightly mobbed by his delighted teammates. While the substitutes were still getting used to the pace of the game, Peru's number 10 made it 3–1, with his second strike a stunning free-kick with the outstep of his right boot. MacLeod had no changes left. In those days only two subs were allowed, and the game finished without addition to the score. What the woefully underprepared Scottish team and large sections of the British media had failed to notice before the game was that the Copa America champions were rather good and in Cubillas, had a deadly marksman. At least the group's other game of the night went as expected with Netherlands bettering Iran 3–0.

Whilst some of the Tartan Army resplendent in kilts and, well, tartan, were disheartened, others remained upbeat. The travelling fans had been taken into the hearts of the locals despite, or perhaps in part, what had happened at Wembley on June 4, 1977. At the time each year, the four home nations of England, Scotland, Wales and Northern Ireland played the British International Championship to decide the UK champions. That year, the Scots had beaten their hosts 2–1 to clinch the title for the second year running. Jubilant fans from north of the border invaded the pitch and left with the ultimate souvenir that not even the Manchester United or Real Madrid club shops had thought of. They went home, or attempted to at least, with one of the crossbars. The ex-Scotland international Denis Law, who is the country's joint top scorer along with Kenny Dalglish, was at a London tube station when he bumped into a group of fans with said crossbar, intent on taking it with them on the tube. Later that night in the Scottish port of Aberdeen, three of the two penalty spots were found for sale.

This is a day I will remember for the rest of my life but not for footballing reasons. I was at a wedding, much to my disappointment. I would have much rather been at home watching the football, and for no apparent reason was attacked by two other children. As one held my arms, the other rushed at me, so I kicked out and forced my assailant back for a moment. However, it was not long enough for me to escape the grip of the much bigger and stronger kid pinning my arms behind my back. As the second attacker ran in again, I tried the same move but this time he saw it coming and grabbed my foot. The next thing I knew I was saying hello to the concrete face first and smashing my two front teeth. Perhaps this was another reason Jordan was one of my favourite players.

MacLeod, who had not gone to watch any of his team's first-round opponents, stating he would rather concentrate on preparing his team, remarked after the defeat that "Our main fault lay in not marking Cubillas", much as a drowning man might have stated that he wished he had learnt to swim. In recent years, the Scottish FA's website has published a poll of the fifty greatest players to ever represent the proud nation. On the list, Souness and Gemmill occupy eighth and ninth respectively. Masson and Ricoh, neither of which would ever pull on the dark blue of their country after Argentina, do not register on the list whatsoever. These were not the only two from this trip to never play for Scotland again. Willie Johnston also ended his international career on Argentinian soil but for a completely different reason.

Drugs Cheat

The West Bromwich Albion winger along with Kenny Dalglish were the two Scots who took the after-game drug test. While the man who would go on to be Scotland's record cap holder was all clear, Johnston was not. He had taken a couple of Reactivan hay fever pills before the game which contained the banned stimulant fencamfamin. Soon the newspaper headlines were screaming about 'drug cheat Johnston'. He was sent home and at least in the eyes of the press, in disgrace. If Scotland had not started their campaign with a loss, would the Scottish FA have sent him packing or would they have stood up for their man who put the event down to a genuine error rather than a Ben Johnson-like effort to cheat. Or was it just too convenient an opportunity to divert attention and say look over here, while they moved the ball around under the cups? Willie must have had that 'why me' feeling, as when the players discussed what had happened amongst themselves, it became clear one or two other players had also taken the same tablet. This is something he has had to live with, but if he had listened to Argentina's Leopoldo Luque, he would not have had to suffer this ordeal.

The Scots had gone on a tour of South America in 1977. Sandwiched between beating Chile 4–2 and going down 2–0 to Brazil they held Argentina to a 1–1 draw. Johnston had a running battle with the host's full-back Vicente Pernia, who at one point spat in the Scotsman's face and before the ninety minutes was up, both men would receive their marching orders. After the game, Luque told the West Brom man not to come back to Argentina, but of course a player who had made his international debut back in 1965 and had not played at a World Cup before (he was not part of the Scottish set-up in 1974) was not going to miss what would probably be his last chance of playing on the biggest stage at the age of thirty-one. I am only guessing, but I think he may now have taken Luque's advice to heart and I doubt if any of the Johnston family holidays have been wine-tasting trips to Mendoza or sightseeing in Buenos Aires. In fact, I wonder if he would even consider accepting a BBQ invite if he realised how important an 'asado' is in Argentinian culture.

Less than a week in and two of the Brits had already been sent home.

Military Junta

On June 6 the teams began the second round of games. Goal-wise, it was the most prolific day in the initial stages of the competition. I witnessed my first World Cup drubbing when reigning champions West Germany demolished Mexico 6–0, a game shown on BBC after 'The Germans' episode of the comedy series *Fawlty Towers*, with some swift attacking football that included a goal that appeared to be written up by

John Cleese himself. Mexico had an attacking free-kick that they managed to get so wrong that Karl-Heinz Rummenigge stole the ball and a few seconds later found himself in the Mexican penalty box, before slotting it under keeper Reyes. To add insult to injury, the Mexican custodian was hurt so badly whilst trying to prevent the goal, he had to be replaced.

However, the real drama was reserved for that day's late game when the hosts faced France, requiring a draw to maintain any hope of progressing alive. The scoring was opened by La Albiceleste skipper Daniel Passarella, with a thumping penalty, the awarding of which till this day will still be met with a shake of the head in France, and although Michel Platini equalised with his first goal at a major tournament, it was not enough as the home side ran out 2–1 winners. The game had many decisions that appeared to go in favour of Argentina, including a far stronger penalty appeal from the French, but many felt there was far more at play than just a 'homer' referee.

It has been alleged that in the post-game urine tests one of the Argentinian players appeared to be pregnant and no action was taken. Tall tale or dirty deeds being discovered? Whichever is the truth, what is not in doubt is that this era was a dark stain on the country's history.

If you look back at old footage now, you will notice the foot of the posts were painted with a black band. This was in fact the equivalent of black armbands. Argentina were awarded the World Cup back in the 1960s but in 1976 the country underwent a military coup which would usher in some of the nation's darkest days. Of course, as a young football fan I was blissfully unaware of this and while some outside the country raised concerns, others who must have had some idea of what was happening pretended to be as innocent as I was.

Two of the world's best players did not travel to Argentina. Germany's Paul Breitner and Johan Cruyff missed the tournament, although thirty years later the Dutchman said his real reason for not going was not a protest but that he had endured a kidnapping attempt at his Barcelona apartment.

At the opening ceremony, the leader of the military junta, General Jorge Rafael Videla, announced the tournament would be played under a sign of peace, with less conviction than a fat man at 2:00 a.m. telling you he is only going to order a salad in the kebab shop. The junta saw this as a chance to show the world a clean face and success became imperative to the regime, a sort of affirmation that they and they alone were right, distracting attention away from their murderous intentions domestically. Videla, although not a football fan himself, was very aware of the positive vibes winning the World Cup would bring to the average Argentinian in the street whilst also strengthening his tyrannical grip on the nation.

In a particularly cruel twist of fate, one of the junta's most notorious torture centres, the Naval Mechanics School, was within a mile of the Monumental stadium in Buenos Aires and it is said the poor souls incarcerated within could hear the cheers resounding from the matches.

Two years before the tournament, rebels opposed to the junta, or Montoneros, assassinated General Omar Actis whilst travelling to a press conference. He was head of the country's World Cup organising committee.

These were not rebels without a cause, for during the seven-year reign of terror it is estimated thirty thousand people were killed. If you did not conform to the regime's ideals you made yourself a target and could easily become one of 'the disappeared' and possibly meet your fate by being thrown out of a plane.

Even if you were part of the government you were not immune if you did or said the wrong thing, as Juan Aleman, the Minister of Finance, would find out. He had criticised the cost of the tournament and during Argentina's notorious game against Peru—more on that later—just as the fourth goal went in, a bomb went off at his house. It was a present from Admiral Massera.

In 1977 a group called *Las Madres de Plaza Mayor*, the Mothers of the Plaza de Mayo, formed by women who had lost children to the junta's 'Dirty War', came into being. This was a brave and dangerous calling as some of the mothers, who every Thursday would march to the Casa Rosada presidential palace holding photos of the offspring they were desperate to see again or at least know the fate of, would themselves become 'the disappeared' and be reunited with their children in the waters of the River Plate.

In a Trump-style move of name calling, anyone who had the temerity to disagree with their thought process was labelled as *las locas*, or the madwomen. In the Netherlands, Dutch TV would screen a documentary, but largely the world seemed to turn if not a blind eye, at least a blinkered one.

While I appreciate there was no internet or a 24-hour news cycle begging to be filled, surely more could have been done to bring pressure from outside the country to end, or at least modify, the regime. I say modify as often within South and Central America the omnipresence of the United States had a hand in their ascension to power. What is good for Uncle Sam is good for the world. Right?

Double Header

Another day, another double header for me, with Brazil versus Spain followed by Scotland against the group minnows and rank outsiders Iran. Brazil again failed to win, drawing with the Spaniards, who at the time were not the success story they have been this century. They had not progressed beyond the group stages since 1950. I was starting to wonder why everybody was quite so excited by the team from South America. The good thing was this meant my day could only get better as Scotland were set to stroll to an easy victory. MacLeod made several changes including dispensing with Ricoh and Masson, bringing in Gemmill but not Souness. On punditry duty for ITV was Andy Gray, who had been sent off in Scotland's opening qualifying game for Argentina and had not played for his country since. Sat alongside him in a shirt that appeared to belong to his little brother was Kevin Keegan. The pair of them had haircuts that reminded me of glam rockers. They both were confident of a Scottish victory and urged them to go for goals. Easier said than done as Scotland turned in a first half performance in which their passing was so bad, it appeared that MacLeod had just picked a starting XI from the travelling fans rather than eleven of the nation's finest.

Still, they managed to go into the break one up. An innocuous ball into the box and Joe Jordan challenged a lost cause which somehow led to some 'Keystone Cops' defending. The Iranian defender Andranik Eskandarian collided with his keeper and with Jordan, the nearest player in a Scottish jersey struggling to get to his feet, decided to swing his left boot at the ball and swept it into his own net from beyond the penalty spot. It was a truly bizarre own goal and thus became the trick answer to the question "Who was the first player from Persia to score at a World

Cup?" Scotland had a goal lead at half-time against the team that would eventually be classified as finishing 14 out of 16 when in 1986 FIFA published rankings for all the previous tournaments. Surely, they could now build on this lead, or at least hold on for a slim victory?

No, they could not, and on the hour mark, Iraj Danaeifard bustled past Gemmill, before beating Alan Rough at his near post, who treated us to a spot of net minding that would reinforce the impression of Scottish goalkeepers being less use than a chocolate fireguard. The game ended 1–1 and with the group's other two teams also playing out a draw, this left Scotland's chances of progressing to the second round on a knife edge.

I don't recall another game until Scotland took on the Netherlands and if you are a similar age to me, you will know why. The match, that has even made it into the movies, will live with me forever. I don't remember seeing Brazil beat Austria to pick up their first victory although I am sure I did due to the agreement with my parents, one I am certain they had begun to regret, with Brazil and Scotland playing all their group games on the same day. I do not remember France playing against Hungary in a dead rubber, bedecked in the green and white shirts of a local club team. We have all forgotten our PE kit at one time or another, forcing us to wear something from the 'lost property' box that just did not feel, look or smell right but I never thought I would see the whole class doing it in unison. Up step France. At a World Cup, no less. Both teams had turned up in their white away kits, Hungary correctly so but the French had made a mistake. Yes, initially they had been told to wear white, but FIFA changed their minds and sent word that the French should revert to their home kit of blue. Unfortunately, Henri Patrelle, who was tasked with the seemingly simple but nonetheless important matter of the national team wearing the correct kit for a game on the world's biggest stage, read FIFA's instructions so carelessly I can only imagine his local fromagerie called to say his favourite cheese had arrived and he must come and collect it now as they were about to close. This led to the wrong colour shirts being brought to Mar de Plata and the correct kit over 200 miles away in Buenos Aires. The referee had no choice but to delay the game while a solution was found. One had to be found, this was the World Cup being broadcast around the world. Salvation arrived in the form of local club Atlético Kimberley who were willing to loan their green and white striped shirts. However, there was still one problem: they did not have numbers on them and they would need to be ironed on. So, a bit of frantic housework and the game kicked off forty minutes late; however, this would cause problems with the television schedule in the UK. *The Good Life* was due to be shown directly after the game and as anybody who has ever watched even one episode knows, Margo is not a woman to be trifled with. The BBC left the game at the interval so the Leadbetters and the Goods could be beamed into our lounges on time, a decision I am certain my parents would have approved of, as this was a programme not to be missed in the seventies. This was just not any episode, it was the last one ever and on top of that, it was a special performance in front of none other than Her Majesty the Queen, another lady whom it would be unwise to upset.

Archie Gemmill

On Sunday June 11, Ally's all but defeated army found itself in Mendoza at the foothills of the Andes to face the Netherlands and their toughest opponent to date.

The manager had reinstated skipper Ricoh and had eventually fallen in line with the view of so many of the pundits and public and was starting the evening with both Gemmill and Souness, the latter of which must have felt like the little Dutch boy with his finger in the dike.

If both Iran and Scotland could upset the odds and win, all four teams in the group would end up on three points meaning goal difference would come into play. Scotland, who so far in one hundred and eighty minutes of football had scored two goals, one of those an own goal, and missed a penalty whilst shipping four at the other end, had to better tonight's far superior opponents by three clear goals in half that time, whilst Iran was looking at a similar mountain.

Scotland started well, appearing to have finally realised where they were and the importance of the game. An unmarked Ricoh hit the bar with a header within the first five minutes. Within ten Johan Neeskens had been stretched off weakening the Dutch midfield and the fact that Dalglish looked more threatening in the initial stages than the whole of the two previous games meant hope, however slim, stayed alive for the Scots.

The team in dark blue even had the ball in the net twice in the opening exchanges.

First was Forsyth from around the penalty spot and although the referee had blown for offside before he shot, he appeared to be onside; possibly one of his teammates had strayed into an offside position, but it was close.

Shortly after, Dalglish thought he had scored after a long punt up field from keeper Rough, only for it to be disallowed in what appeared an even harsher decision than the previous one.

Then ten minutes before the break everything reverted to type. Stuart Kennedy gave away a penalty and Archie Gemmill managed to get his name taken. Robbie Rensenbrink beat Alan Rough with the resulting spot-kick to score the thousandth goal in World Cup history.

Just before half-time things looked up, Dalglish getting just rewards for his first stanza efforts when he buried a knockdown from Jordan; immediately after that the Dutch had to replace an injured Rijsbergen.

It was 1–1 with forty-five minutes left but the way Scotland had played meant that although it was still mission improbable it was not mission impossible. The two first half injuries suffered by the Netherlands meant their Austrian coach Ernst Happel, who would go on to be recognised as one of the greatest coaches in the history of the game and after his death have a stadium named after him in his home country, had no cards left to play after his interval team talk. MacLeod was still holding a full deck as the second half started, an event which the BBC managed to miss.

Within short order the Scots had won a penalty when Souness was fouled. This time Gemmill was given the responsibility from 12 yards out and proved up to the task with a precise shot into the corner: 2–1 and two more needed.

And then it happened. Halfway through the second half brought that goal, the goal that meant Scotland only needed one more, but it was so much more than that, it was a moment in Scottish footballing history.

Scotland have never progressed beyond the initial stages at any finals, so for them this one moment in the South American sun was the equivalent of Brazil's third triumph or Spain eventually claiming the trophy after so many promising tournaments had ended in failure.

So iconic that twenty years later it found its way into a sex scene in Irvine Welsh's *Trainspotting*, it has been the inspiration for a dance piece and inevitably been recreated on *Fantasy Football League* by Frank Skinner and David Baddiel.

Gemmill was first to a loose ball and in a matter of seconds had left three of his opponents on the ground while he jumped, jinked and gyrated towards the Dutch goal, before lifting the ball over the Dutch custodian and oldest player at these finals, Jan Jongbloed; 3–1. Twenty-two minutes and one more goal needed. Within a minute Scotland came within a whisker of scoring an own goal and the simple fact that they had managed to avoid shooting themselves in the foot meant it felt like they would be able to accomplish their monumental task.

For the next couple of minutes my dad raved about Gemmill's goal like I had never heard him before or after, but then of course it happened. The Scottish defence left a hole the size of the Hebrides which Johnny Rep gleefully ran into before unleashing a screamer from 25 yards out to reduce the deficit to one. While the Dutch celebrated, Gemmill could be seen massaging his face as if he was rubbing a lamp, looking for an elusive genie to give him two more wishes and two more goals. Alas it was not to be. Scotland were out despite a magnificent 3–2 victory as MacLeod chose to finish with his eleven starters rather than make any changes.

The team that had left Scotland with swagger, bluster and the hopes of a nation and those of a little boy had been found out; they were just not that good. Or were they? They had, after all, played extremely well in defeating the Dutch and amongst their numbers could call upon four of the country's ten greatest-ever players, according to the aforementioned Scottish FA list. As well as the players ranked eight and nine the man in tenth place, Joe Jordan, was also an integral part of this team, as was the player voted into top spot, Kenny Dalglish.

Overhyped or underachievers? I guess only that small group of men that left Hampden to such fanfare can really answer that.

Second Group Stages

Unlike World Cups of today, instead of knockout rounds, the teams that qualified went into two more groups, the winners of which would contest the final. Group A was the European group and consisted of Netherlands, Austria, Italy and West Germany, whilst Group B became known as the South American group and was made up of Argentina, Brazil, Peru plus a sole team from Europe, Poland. The significance of the fact that Argentina always played their match after the day's other game in their section had been wrapped up was only unclear to those without a Machiavellian heart.

The two finalists would not be decided until the last round of the group games, all played on the same day, providing not only a hatful of goals and excitement, but also controversy that still divides a continent to this day.

Italy looked to be the first nation heading to the final when they went into the break versus the Netherlands with a one goal lead, due to an Ernie Brandts' own goal from outside his own box. In the same phase of play he slid into Piet Scrhrijvers, the Dutch goalie, who had to be stretchered off and replaced by Jan Jongbloed. A few minutes after the break, Brandts scored his second goal of the day, again from outside of the box, this time at the right end. In doing so he became the first player to score for both teams in a finals match.

With the score at 1–1, up stepped Arie Hann. In a tournament full of fantastic strikes from distance with the likes of Boniek, Dirceu and Cubilllas, treating us to spectacular goals, Hann's was the cream of the crop. It was an astonishing strike, which I still remember as if it were yesterday, for the game's third and final goal, all scored from outside the penalty area to send the Oranje to their second successive final. With Group A settled, Brazil took on the Netherlands and due to a misreading of the *Radio Times* magazine it looked for one awful moment that I would miss my second Brazil game in a row; they previously played Argentina in a 0–0 draw, a game deemed too late at night for me to watch. At first my mum had declared that the Brazil versus Poland tie was going to clash with *Morecambe and Wise*, so I was going to miss out. On further inspection of the TV schedule, this proved to be an error and after forty-five minutes of laughter, I got to watch my game. Brazil ran out 3–1 winners meaning that either they or the hosts would face off against Holland four days later. Argentina had to better Peru by four clear goals, otherwise the most successful team in World Cup history would be playing in the final for the fourth time in the last six tournaments and at their expense.

Grains, Gains and Goals

The final games of the first round had given us excitement and goals aplenty and while the final game of the second round served up plenty more goals, excitement was surpassed by accusations of skulduggery and machinations that still rumble today.

Now, the advantage of playing their game an hour after Brazil had finished their tie with Poland became crystal clear; La Albiceleste knew exactly what they needed to do.

Despite the fact that whatever the result Peru could not progress, the passionate crowd in the packed stadium in Rosario nearly saw Los Incas take the lead when they hit the post while the tie was still at 0–0. Mario Kempes then opened the scoring for the home side. Shortly before the interval Alberto Tarantini doubled the lead with his only international goal, one that Peru's Argentinian-born goalkeeper Quiroga should have saved. Was he 'helping' the land of his birth'? Or was it just a similar mistake to the one he made against Brazil, which also led to a goal? At the final whistle, a 6–0 score-line saw Argentina comfortably through to their first final since the very first tournament. But was all as it seemed? Or was it, as many maintain, a fix?

In the bowels of the stadium before the game something strange had occurred. The Argentinian dictator, General Jorge Rafael Videla, visited the Peruvian dressing room, which is unusual enough in itself, but he was accompanied, according to several of the Peruvian team, by former US Secretary of State, Dr Henry Kissinger. The American was known to be a big football fan, but had no recollection of this meeting later on.

What was the purpose of this visit at a time when Peru was also under a military regime? Was it just a 'look at me moment' to remind the players of what could happen to those that upset the rulers of the two countries in the era of Operation Condor, a campaign of political regression and state terror carried out by several South American countries under right-wing dictatorships with alleged support from the United States? Or was it just a show of South America brotherhood with Videla, so blinded by power he did not consider the optics?

What was alleged for a long time was that 35,000 tonnes of grain were shipped from Argentina to Peru in exchange for the home side getting the result they needed, but that is by far not the only theory. In a 1998 interview with La Nación, the Peruvian stopper Quiroga pointed his gloved hand at the referee saying *"Pienso que estaba retocado"*, or that the man in the middle had been subject to outside influences. He also suggested some of his teammates may have accepted bribes. Years later, another player from the match, Jose Velasquez, would also accuse six of his teammates of accepting bribes. Velasquez, at the time one of Peru's key players, is still baffled why he was chosen to be substituted shortly into the second half, but what may have slipped his mind was the score was already 4–0 and he had received a yellow card. Two Peruvian players, Cubiillas and Chumpitaz, did admit to being offered financial compensation, not from the hosts, but from Brazil, if they prevented Argentina from reaching the final.

Some argue that the proof Los Incas did throw the game lies in the fact that they were wearing their second strip so as not to stain the national jersey. This was just in line with FIFA protocols of having one team in light colours and the other in dark and Argentina being hosts would not be the team to wear the second strip.

In 2012 came yet another accusation and not just from a tabloid looking for an easy headline but from a special court set up to investigate human rights abuses. This was far more sinister than money or grain being paid for a favourable result. This time the voice belonged to former Peruvian senator Genaro Ledesma. He ascertains that the government of his country under the direction of President Morales Bermudez had him, along with other political prisoners, shipped to Argentina for the dictatorship to 'disappear' them in exchange for the right result on the football field, an event that has led to him calling for the outcome of the '78 World Cup to be annulled.

Was the gulf in class really that big? While Argentina up to this point had scored no more than two goals in any game in the tournament, whilst only keeping two clean sheets in five outings, they had under Menotti's reign played Peru four times, winning all of them. Additionally, they had recorded two 5–1 victories (over Hungary and Venezuela), scored six against the USA without reply and humbled Venezuela again by a mammoth 11–0 score-line during his rule. So yes, they could run up big scores, but under Menotti in two attempts they had never gotten past the group stages of the Copa America and even with the addition of Maradona, lost three of their five games at the 1982 World Cup.

Whether it came about through incisive football, pacts between dictators or simply an old-fashioned bribe, they were through to the final.

My First Final

On the evening of June 25 we settled down to watch the final, with David Coleman on the BBC, after what my mum would call 'party' food which we would often have on a Sunday. It was sandwiches, always ham and tomato, pork pies, biscuits and home-made iced fairy cakes. I have no idea what was available in British supermarkets back then, but my mum was a simple cook and nothing as exotic as chorizo or quiche ever made it into her shopping trolley.

With a full tummy and head bursting with excitement, I could not wait for the game to start, but I would have to. Firstly, Argentina came out late, letting the Dutch stew in front of seventy thousand intimidating fans packed into River Plate's El Monumental Stadium. Once the two teams were on the ticker tape-covered pitch, more controversy broke out involving the hosts. This time, just before the game was due to kick-off, Argentina's captain Daniel Passarella decided this was the appropriate time to object to Rene van der Kerkhof's plaster protecting a broken bone in his wrist. He had permission from FIFA and he had worn it for most of the tournament without incident. At one point, with the Dutch looking like they were going to walk off, a solution was found by adding another layer of bandage, but the Argentinian captain's underhanded plan had worked. The Dutch concentration was as shot to pieces as Bonnie, Clyde and their V8 Ford on that fateful day in Louisiana. Additionally, I suspect Argentina now knew the referee was pliable and not likely to go against them on any contentious decisions in front of such a vociferous crowd.

This was not the first stroke the home side had pulled since advancing to the final. The referee should have been Israeli Abraham Klein, but the home side objected, ostensibly because of the ties between the two nations. The real probable reason? He had overseen the host's only defeat of the tournament so far, to Italy, and had shown an iron will not to be intimidated by the spectators, something others entrusted with the whistle had failed to do when faced with the baying home crowd. This would not do, so he was replaced with Italy's Sergio Gonella, with the whole of Argentina deftly sidestepping the fact that there were strong links between these two nations.

Eventually, belatedly, Argentina kicked off the biggest game in world football and for the first time in the tournament, I would get to watch them live. Thankfully it was long before the days of the internet and 24-hour sports channels, so if you missed a live game, you could often watch the highlights without knowing the result.

Argentina drew first blood when *El Matador*, Mario Kempes, fired in the opener, a goal that drew him level with Teófilo Cubillas and Rob Rensenbrink (who was starting for the Dutch) in the race to be the tournament's top marksman. The Netherlands equalised during the last ten minutes and in a game full of bad tackles and dirty tricks, Passarella took out Johan Neeskens with a right hand that should have seen him see red, with the score at 1–1. With the clock showing just past forty-five minutes played in the second period, a free-kick from within the Dutch half fell to Rensenbrink, who in an agonising moment for all those in orange, rolled the ball against the post when it looked for all the world that he would score. Shortly after, the ref blew for full-time.

My first World Cup had been extended by thirty minutes. Thirty minutes that I really hoped the Dutch could take advantage of and win for the first time. Alas, Kempes made it 2–1 before Daniel Bertoni added a third for Argentina when the competition's top scorer had lost control of the ball and it had fallen to his teammate. Although Kempes, as only a striker could do, has since claimed he was about to score and that the Argentinian number 4 had denied him a hat-trick.

Was it a victory owed to great play and excellent preparation? The squad had been training together since February, apart from Kempes, who was the only squad member to play his club football outside Argentina. He had been the last player allowed to be transferred out of the country who had a shot of making the squad, before a transfer embargo was put in place at Menotti's behest.

Or was it a trophy won with bribes and threats? We will probably never know as Videla died in prison in 2013.

SPAIN 1982

England at Last

Although by 1982 I had seen England play in a major tournament, the poorly received 1980 European Championship, I still longed to see my country perform on the biggest stage. In a tight qualifying group, one night in 1981 in Budapest, the whole country saw my dream come a little closer: emerging 3–1 victors to go top of their group, from which two teams would qualify, with the goals being scored by two of the most influential players in the team, Kevin Keegan with a penalty and a Trevor Brooking brace. The second of Brooking's goals memorably lodged itself between the net support and the inside of the post. Ron Greenwood's men now had only two games to play, away to Norway, followed by the last game of the section at home to that night's vanquished foes.

The September visit to Oslo could not roll around quickly enough for me, a game in which victory for the away side was all but ensured. England had faced the group minnows on five previous occasions winning all five handsomely, including a 4–0 victory in the group's opening game.

Well, every English football fan can tell you what happened next: a 2–1 defeat after being one up and a Norwegian commentary that has gone into folklore. At the end of the game with the home crowd on the pitch mobbing their unlikely heroes, Bjorge Lillelien, switching admirably back and forth between Norwegian and English, taunted famous English figures including, but not limited to, Lord Nelson, Sir Winston Churchill, Henry Cooper and Lady Diana before his never to be forgotten "Your boys took a hell of a beating", which was directed squarely at British Prime Minister, Maggie Thatcher. The result meant England needed to rely on other nations dropping points, so the all-too-real prospect of England missing a third World Cup in a row reared its ugly head. It was a thought that did not bear entertaining especially for those a few years older than me that could remember the 1974 finals.

However, by the time the game with Hungary transpired, things had gone England's way, with the 'home of football' only needing to draw with the Hungarians, who had an unassailable lead at the top of the section and knew they would be playing in España '82 whatever the outcome on the night. Paul Mariner scored the only goal of the game early on for the home side, meaning the England team, like many in the British Isles did every year, would be heading to Spain.

The farcical draw that was made in Madrid in January was the biggest to date, containing twenty-four teams who would contest fifty-two games in just under a month. It included two other British representatives, Northern Ireland and for the third tournament in a row, Scotland. Using big mechanical cages that were normally used for the Spanish lottery that often broke down, Scotland were at one point mistakenly placed in the wrong section, while back in the British studios, several players hoping to star in Spain, such as Keegan, Souness, Alan Hansen and Pat Jennings, looked on with quiet bemusement.

No Opening Game

England, fifth favourites behind the hosts and the last three champions headed south to Bilbao, and despite failing to win their group, were one of the seeded teams playing all their group games in one city. This was, at least in part, due to the hooliganism problem that dogged English football at the time. It was apparently easier for the authorities to control things in one place. The Irish made their way to Zaragoza and Valencia, whilst the Scots travelled to Seville and Malaga, as each group's games would be held over just two venues to minimise travelling for the teams and supporters, as opposed to today's multi-venue groups.

At home, things had changed; we had been transformed from a one television family to a three-set household. The front of our house was an extension onto the existing structure, so my bedroom had the strange aspect of having windows that looked out to our front room. This had previously just been used as a dining area, yet now had a large ceramic-style bar added with a pool table along with a second colour TV. In April, for my fifteenth birthday, I had been given a small black-and-white portable one for my room by my parents, I guess with the upcoming tournament in mind.

Cameroon, Honduras and New Zealand were amongst the first-time qualifiers whilst Netherlands and Mexico were two of those from Argentina that missed out.

The latest that games started in Spain was 9:00 p.m. local time, meaning they were a family friendly 8:00 p.m. on British television. Despite this and possibly because of the increased number of participants and therefore lack of rest days, the television coverage was not as comprehensive as four years earlier, with no daytime round-ups shown and some first-round games not shown live, even if they did not clash with another game. Also, the image of hooliganism may have affected some TV executive's thoughts, something Paul Gascoigne would have a great bearing on eight years later.

With all this choice of viewing devices, I still managed to miss not only the opening game but the second game as well.

The opener pitched Argentina as defending champions against Belgium and while ITV had the rights to show it, they decided not to broadcast Diego Maradona's World Cup debut, fearing a backlash due to an ongoing squabble over some sheep-infested rocks in the North Atlantic, or as it is more commonly known, 'The Falklands War' between Britain and our old friend the Argentinian military junta. This turned out to be a mistake, as for the first time since 1962, an opening game at the finals produced a goal. It was only one, but the one was for Belgium, for which I am sure anybody with anti-Argentina sentiment would have cheered loudly, whilst those of us who accepted the conflict was an entirely separate issue to a game of football, would have happily just watched the match.

Since 1978, I had changed from 'little school' to 'big school' which was in the city of Salisbury instead of the next village. Although the last bell of the day rang at 3.55 p.m. and we only lived 7 miles away if you took the direct route, our coach would sometimes not pick us up for another half an hour. Living in the small settlement of Lopcombe Corner, we were always the last to be dropped off, sometimes as late as 6:00 p.m., so the 4.15 p.m. UK start time of Italy versus Poland came and went without me settled in front of it.

With three British teams to follow, I eagerly checked the group kick-off times and thankfully discovered that all of Scotland and Northern Ireland's were in the late slot, but all three of England's were early starts. Disaster. After a quick chat and a lot of persuasion, it was agreed Mum would pick me up from school on these days, so I could be at home in time to see the first ball kicked in each of their ties.

The first game I saw live was Brazil versus the Soviet Union, with the Eastern Europeans taking the lead thanks to some atrocious goalkeeping by the Brazilian net minder, before the Selecao struck back with two superb strikes. One from Socrates, a qualified physician and the other from Eder, a qualified pain in the arse for many of his managers, for a 2–1 victory. The World Cup was back for me.

The Brits Are Here

First up of the British representatives was Scotland who started off rather better than four years earlier, going in at half-time three goals to the good against New Zealand. Then the inevitable case of the 'Scottywobbles' took hold of a team that was now under the stewardship of Jock Stein and within twenty minutes of the restart, the rank outsiders had pulled the score back to 2–3 and it took two late set-piece goals to give the Scots a flattering 5–2 victory. One of the starting line-up that day may surprise younger readers who only know him as TalkSPORT's bon vivant and for a long time the sensible, well, maybe voice of reason is a better description, half of a double act with Mike 'Porky' Parry. Alan Brazil was the youngest member of the Scottish squad turning twenty-three on the very day of his World Cup bow. I would wager this may have been one of his more sober birthdays.

I woke to find that Scotland's game had been relatively low scoring compared to the night's other game, Hungary setting a World Cup record with a 10–1 blitzing of El Salvador. This was of no importance to me, as today England were set to take on France. As I came out of school, I eagerly scanned the parked cars looking for Mum's blue-and-white Austin A60, and there it was, as promised. There were other kids who, on the odd occasion I would get picked up from school, would try and cadge a lift and normally I would try and persuade my parents to drop them off. However, as they approached the car Mum did not have to say anything, a "no way" from a teenager in a hurry was all they got this time.

Luckily my school was in Laverstock on the edge of Salisbury, so once we had driven the short distance to the A30 it was one straight road back to our house, although this did not stop me haranguing my mother to "press the pedal on the right a little harder" and to overtake at the slightest opportunity. In my defence, Mum could be a particularly slow driver. She would say careful, but no, the correct word was definitely slow and a complete contrast to my dad. Although he had now not competed for several years, he had raced Mini Coppers all over the UK at tracks such as Brands Hatch, Silverstone and Thruxton. He obviously missed the adrenaline rush as he treated the road as one giant racetrack, but alas, he was normally still at work when I was in need of speedy chauffeuring services. We made it back in time for a game in which it turned out vital to see the first ball kicked for any Englishman, especially those of us who did not remember 1970.

In the glorious Spanish sunshine, during the very first minute, a Steve Coppell throw-in was headed on by Terry Butcher into the path of my favourite player, alongside many other Manchester United fans, Bryan Robson, who somehow got his left foot to the ball to score the World Cup's fastest goal on twenty-seven seconds. If I had been taken in by Ally MacLeod four years earlier about the Scots' chances, I now had the evidence of my own eyes telling me this World Cup thing, once you got there, was easy and that I would be watching England lift the trophy on July 11.

France equalised but a second from Robson—he also was always going to be the tournament's top marksman—and another from Paul Mariner meant England won 3–1. The group's other two teams faced off the following day and little fancied Kuwait held Czechoslovakia to a draw as things got even better for the Three Lions.

Now, before anybody tells me I have made a mistake saying Robson's was the fastest World Cup goal ever, just delete that tweet because to anybody of my age it was, despite Vaclav Masek's 1962 goal after sixteen seconds for Czechoslovakia and a Peter Platzer effort after twenty-four seconds way back in 1934.

At the time, all the media outlets reported it as the fastest goal, FIFA even presenting the Manchester United star with a gold watch to mark his achievement. It was only years later that this mistake was rectified when FIFA decided to time some old footage and of course in 2002, all of this was made redundant when Hakan Suker netted for Turkey against South Korea after just eleven seconds.

The day of the game against France was a cloudless, breezeless, scorching hot one in Bilbao. After the game, it turned out that the England team had lost six stones in weight between them. Paul Mariner was slimming champion, losing 11lbs. Whilst the polyester strip was popular with the fans, the players found that the sweat during the game clung to the shirts and did not repel the heat. Action was needed. A call was made to strip manufacturer Admiral, a company that had begun its life as a small underwear manufacturer in Leicester, until a chance meeting with then Leeds manager Don Revie led to them becoming a major football kit supplier, asking for a solution. Overnight they miraculously produced five kits per player to the individual sizes required. Designer Debbie Jackson then drove to Manchester airport with the shirts in the back of her Polo. Once there she sat in a hotel room painstakingly sewing new badges onto each shirt. If you look closely at England's next game against Czechoslovakia you will notice, unsurprisingly, that they were not sewn on in a uniform fashion.

At the same time as England played France, one of the biggest shocks in World Cup history was taking place. European champions West Germany were taking on debutants Algeria, playing in their first World Cup. The German coach Jupp Derwell was so confident of victory that if his team lost, he said he would "jump on the first train back to Munich". After a goalless first half, the Africans took the lead nine minutes after the break, Karl-Heinz Rummenigge equalising midway through the second stanza to apparently save his manager checking the train timetables from Gijon to Bavaria. Before the Germans could build on this, Algeria hit back immediately with a fine team goal turned home from within the six-yard box by African footballer of the Year Lakhdar Belloumi, to give them the game 2–1. Always one to support the underdog, watching the highlights of this after England's victory really put me in a good mood, as I settled down to my homework. Being in the top set meant I had a bit every night, but luckily, we had some teachers that were sympathetic and gave us longer than normal during the tournament. Others were not quite as switched on when it came to dealing with a school full of teenage boys. "It's just some grown men kicking a pig's bladder around a field" was trotted out on more than one occasion by some grown men who just ended up kicking themselves when even the most diligent students did not get their homework in on time. Our geography teacher was an Irishman with a quick temper and an even quicker wrist when he threw the blackboard rubber at any child with a real or perceived lack of attention. I thought the World Cup was a great way of teaching geography—maybe each kid could take a qualified nation and write about them—but nobody spoke to Mr Bradshaw unless they had absolutely no choice, so the idea of suggesting lesson planning to him quickly came and went. Although I must give him credit for never singling out any pupil because of their background, appearance or academic ability. Instead, he appeared to hate all children equally.

Give It Your Best

The next day saw the final British participants kick-off their campaign when Northern Ireland, with thirty-seven-year-old Pat Jennings in goal, drew 0–0 with Yugoslavia, nearly two decades after he had made his international debut alongside George Best. In the build-up to the tournament there was a campaign for Irish manager Billy Bingham to include the mercurial Irishman, but unlike Jennings, who was an integral part of the qualifying campaign, Bestie had not pulled on the green of Ireland since 1977, last scoring an international goal six years previously when he treated the Windsor Park fans to a hat-trick, as his team cruised to a 5–0 victory against Cyprus. At club level the two icons of Irish football had taken wildly differing paths. Jennings was still playing at the top level of English football while George spent the early eighties playing for a poor team in a poor North American soccer league. In fact, after leaving Manchester United in the mid-seventies, he never played at anything approaching elite level on the domestic front, with the 1968 European Cup being the last trophy he would ever claim. It would have been great to see him light it up a World Cup but by this stage of his career all he could light up was a fag.

I am too young to remember a prime Georgie but have seen enough footage to know that if he was given today's pitches with the amount of protection afforded to the more skilful players, he would be leaving school just as Lionel Messi was kissing his mummy goodbye on his first day of kindergarten. However, on display that day was a player who, thanks to his young age, background and club side, was inevitably labelled the 'new George Best'.

At seventeen years and forty-one days, Norman Whiteside broke Pele's longstanding record of being the youngest player to appear at a finals tournament, a record that still stands today. The two players who made their names at Manchester United ended their careers with spookily similar records for their national team. Best scored nine goals in thirty-seven appearances, Whiteside netted exactly the same number whilst playing one more game. Norman played at two World Cups while George, sadly for him and football fans all over the globe, never graced the ultimate stage.

The Brit's games kept coming thick and fast with the Scots taking on Brazil, marking the fifth day in a row of me watching a live game. With it being the late game, I was joined in the front room by my parents. After Scotland took the lead with a David Narey toe poke, my dad, who had not had the benefit of watching England due to being at work and did not watch much football between World Cups, started to talk them up. Four years earlier he was on the verge of boarding the Ally MacLeod delusion special. Brazil soon put that right with a wonderful display of football, especially from two of their star players who stood out, even in this unbelievably talented squad. Wearing the revered number 10 was Zico, along with skipper Socrates. A goal each from Zico, Oscar, Eder, which left Scottish keeper Alan Rough rooted to the spot, and Falcao sealed the win. The captain amazed his teammates not just with his skill or talent but his new-found sudden level of fitness, that was not so sudden at all. In the build-up to Spain, he put himself on a strict five-month fitness regime, along with cutting back on the beer that helped him shed the best part of two stone.

Additionally, the chain smoker was off the cigarettes, now physically as well as mentally a leader of the pack. So impressive was the Brazilian performance that after the game the Scots manager, who had been round the block more than once and looked like he may even have run into it on a couple of occasions, mused, "It will be good for soccer if they win it. It never is easy to accept defeat but this one is different." A magnanimous statement, about as far removed as possible from what his predecessor would have treated us to. Zico's effort would not have been a free-kick,

Oscar's header would have been misdirected, Eder's, well, the wind would have taken that in and Falcao's eighty-seventh minute strike might have been genuine but only because the boys were tired in the Seville heat as it approached 11:00 p.m.

At the same time, defending world champions Argentina defeated Hungary by the same score-line of 4–1, including Maradona's first ever World Cup goal.

Soon England were back in action. This time on a Sunday, so no mad rush home to see a straightforward 2–0 victory over Czechoslovakia, that meant they had qualified for the second round with a game to spare. The only sour note was Bryan Robson having to leave the game at the interval with an injury, but at least he was replaced by one of the finest players of the generation, Glenn Hoddle, at whose England debut I had been present when he scored a spectacular goal against Bulgaria nearly three years earlier. However, neither this fast start to international football nor two successive FA Cup wins with Tottenham Hotspur had convinced Greenwood he should be a regular starter for his country.

France Kuwait Refereed From the Stands

I am not sure how many people saw the highlights of France's 4–1 victory over Kuwait, but I would wager that nobody who managed to predict the right result and all five goal scorers also had added to their betting slip what happened towards the end of the game. Alan Giresse scored to put the French 4–1 up only for the Kuwait team to say they had heard a whistle from the crowd and had thought it came instead from the referee and stopped playing. Miroslav Stupar ruled the goal would stand. That should have been that; sacrosanct to the game until VAR was the fact that the referee's decision is final. We have often seen players remonstrating with the match officials over real or imagined injustices. That day it went a little further. Amongst the thirty-thousand crowd was one man who managed to do what countless footballers down the years have failed to do: force the referee to change his decision. The Kuwaiti Prince Fahed, who was also president of his country's FA—sometimes it is about who you know and not what you know—left the VIP area and staged a royal pitch invasion in his flowing dish-dash. After threats that his side would walk off, the goal was disallowed, much to the annoyance of the French. Eventually the game continued with France scoring at the death to restore the 4–1 score-line. Neither Stupar nor Kuwait have been seen at a World Cup since.

While one debutant was turning not only the neutrals but also the world's garlic farmers against them, another in the form of Algeria had made the headlines for all the right reasons five days earlier, going down 2–0 to Austria with no inkling of how significant that second goal would be. Later that day, Northern Ireland were again held to a draw, a result that meant they would need an improbable win against World Cup hosts Spain to progress.

Scottish Failure

Over the next four days the twelve teams that would be progressing were to be decided. With the majority still capable of going through there was plenty to play for and in similar fashion to four years earlier, the hosts would play the last game of the first section knowing the exact result they needed. However, in a backward step from Argentina, none of each group's games would be played at the same time, always leaving the two teams playing last in each section with the advantage of knowing exactly what result would see them through. It was a decision that would leave FIFA red-faced and should have left two neighbours with even redder ones due to embarrassment, but first of course there was time for some glorious Scottish failure.

In Group 6, Brazil were already safely through with a game to spare, whilst Scotland still had to face the Soviet Union. Both teams had collected two points, but due to the Soviet's superior goal difference only a victory would do for Scotland. Things got off to a good start, Joe Jordan sending them into the break with a 1–0 lead. If they could keep a clean sheet for forty-five minutes, they would be through to the second stage. However, the inevitable equaliser soon came, yet the Scots needed just one goal and with the likes of Steve Archibald, Gordon Strachan and John Robertson on the pitch, they had the attacking talent to supply it. Stein played his final card when he sent on Danny McGrain and Alan Brazil in the seventy-first minute; only two subs were permitted at this World Cup with 1998 being the first to allow a third, and a goal soon came. Unfortunately for Scotland, it was at the wrong end of the pitch.

Willie Miller and Alan Hansen collided with better comedic timing than the Two Ronnies to leave Shengelia a clear run at an abandoned Alan Rough, an opportunity the Georgian-born forward was not going to miss. Hansen would later become a Match of the Day pundit known for describing defending as diabolical, woeful and shocking, I would suggest he had never laid eyes on defending as bad as he and Miller's that day.

Of course, within two minutes the Scots equalised through midfield enforcer Graeme Souness, but with only four minutes left they had done too little too late yet again and had to settle for a 2–2 draw, meaning this was the third World Cup in a row they were sent home on goal difference. Over the three tournaments they had a respectable record of played nine, won three, drew four, whilst losing only twice, one of those to the superb Brazil team in Spain. This was Joe Jordan's swan song for his country and although he only managed eleven goals in fifty-two appearances, over three different finals, he netted four times in seven outings, making him Scotland's leading World Cup marksman.

The games over the next couple of days came and went with teams' fate being decided until only one day and three matches were left to complete the first stage. For the first time I would get to see two of the home nations on the same day. England beat Kuwait 1–0 in an afternoon kick-off and a game I remember little about, but the events of the day's two other matches meant a game that had little riding on it was an easily forgotten contest.

Disgrace of Gijon

At the same time as England were becoming one of only two teams to maintain a 100% winning record in the initial phase, the other being the sublime Brazilian team, one of football's most controversial yet boring games was taking place. Or was it as bad as it was portrayed?

The day before, Algeria had raced into a 3–0 half-time lead against Chile and although the South Americans pulled two back in the second period, this was enough to leave Algeria with four points and a goal difference of zero. This little bit of history, they were the first African nation to win two World Cup games, meant they would have been through in four of five of the other groups.

Group 2's last game was Austria versus West Germany, an age-old football rivalry. Four years earlier in Argentina, in what has been dubbed 'The Miracle of Cordoba', the Austrians ran out winners by the odd goal in five, a thrilling game which was a first victory over their neighbours in forty-seven years that also put an end to their rival's hopes of reaching the final four. If the Germans won by one or two goals, both they and Austria would progress. Any other result meant that only one of the combatants would be staying in Spain.

Horst Hrubesch, who two years earlier had scored both of West Germany's goals as they were crowned champions of Europe against Belgium, opened the scoring on ten minutes to give the crowd hope of another classic, but it never materialised.

My memory of the coverage at the time was that the goal was certain to be the last piece of meaningful action and that neither side crossed the halfway line with much attacking intent for the rest of the game. Reading a report from *The Guardian* newspaper from 2010 reinforces that memory, claiming nothing really happened for the next eighty minutes, with no shots on goal for the rest of the game. Eight years later the same paper printed a different version of events.

The latter report, where the author appears to have actually watched the game, rather than solely rely on sound bites from others, gives a different side to the story. He does agree that the last fifteen minutes is a particularly damp squib; is that really much of a surprise when so close to the end the score-line suited both teams? Yet does recall the ten minutes after the goal as being essentially competitive football and mentions Wolfgang Dremmler's shot during this passage of play being the second and last effort of the ninety minutes to draw a save from either keeper.

After the whistle that indicated the break, one of the German players put an arm around the shoulder of one of his opponents and struck up a conversation. Was this the moment when the result was decided, and the non-aggression pact was formalised? We don't know, but what we do know is that the players would have no problem understanding each other, German being the most widely spoken language in Austria. The second *Guardian* article uses some figures from Opta statistics. In the second half there were only three shots at goal but three there was and that fact alone discredits the earlier report. West Germany only made six tackles and both teams had an extremely high pass completion rate.

After the break, the Spanish crowd let their feelings be known by waving their handkerchiefs, a sign of displeasure in the land of sun and sangria, whilst shouting *"Que se besen"*—let them kiss. The Algerians in the crowd who understandably had more than most to feel aggrieved about started waving not handkerchiefs, but banknotes at the players, while others set light to their spends.

There are reports of Austrian and German commentators calling the game a disgrace, urging TV viewers to turn off or refusing to speak whilst on-air, but how far into the game did all this happen? What also must be remembered is that these are two footballing rivals and many of those watching, especially in Austria, would have wanted to see the other team depart. So 'The Disgrace of Gijon' ended 1–0 and both sides made it safely, if not altogether satisfactorily, through to the last twelve.

Hans Tschak, the head of the Austrian delegation, saw no issues with what had happened. After explaining that it was natural for the game to be played in a tactical fashion, he commented, "But if 10,000 'sons of the desert' here in the stadium want to trigger a scandal because of this, it just goes to show that they have too few schools. Some sheikh comes out of an oasis, is allowed to get a sniff of World Cup air after 300 years and thinks he's entitled to open his gob." Reports that he joined the Austrian diplomatic core after the game proved to be wide of the mark.

Algeria naturally appealed, FIFA held a three-and-a-half-hour meeting, and nothing happened. Well, at least not at this World Cup. From the 1986 finals onwards, the last two matches in each group would have simultaneous kick-off times on the same day; it had only taken FIFA eight years and two scandals, a low number by their standards, to work this out.

Was the result all that surprising? The two teams that met that afternoon had come through the same qualifying group, with the Germans winning by two goals on each occasion, 2–0 at home and 3–1 away. Up until that result in Cordoba, from 1934 on they had faced each other twelve times, the Germans winning nine, with three games ending all square and six of those victories being by a one or two goal margin. They had also played a friendly in 1980 with the Germans coming out on top 1–0. And the most common winning score-line in the first group stage at this World Cup? 1–0.

Irish eyes are smiling

The last game of the initial stages, like four years earlier, featured a British team needing a result against one of the tournament favourites. This time Northern Ireland faced the hosts in Valencia. Spain sat at the head of the group with Yugoslavia second and the Irish in third. Billy Bingham's plan had been to draw with the Yugoslav's, accomplished, beat Honduras, failed, and draw with the Spanish, to be decided.

A draw against Spain was the minimum requirement that balmy evening but it needed to be high scoring—unlikely, but possible. I have seen teams set up for a 0–0 many times but setting out for a 2–2 or 3–3 is an unusual tactic, to say the least. Martin O'Neill, who would go on to make his name in management at Wycombe Wanderers before winning trophies with Leicester and Celtic and in 2013 become the Republic of Ireland's manager, counselled his teammates with Brian Clough-like clarity and simplicity before the game. He suggested the Spanish would come at them and they needed to get behind the ball, make life as difficult as possible for their opponents and that they would gradually get some opportunities. They merely had to put one of them in the back of the net and win 1–0. While the midfielder before the match talked about the tactics, my mum lamented about George Best not being available. Thinking back now I am convinced it had nothing to do with his abilities on the pitch, but far more his looks!

Half-time came and went with no score but shortly after the restart everything changed. Gerry Armstrong picked up a stray Spanish pass deep in his own half before running determinedly at his opponent's goal. About 30 yards out he fed Billy Hamilton who outmuscled his defender and put in a cross that Luía Arconada, who many saw as the best goalkeeper in Europe at the time, could only push out into Armstrong's path. The scorer steadied himself before sending a low hard drive into the Spanish net, for what was the hundredth goal of this World Cup. John Motson informed us that this score put both teams through with what would have been considered an unlikely scenario just a fortnight before of the Irish topping the group, but one more for 'Norn Iron' put the

Spanish out and if it ended 1–1 lots would have to be drawn to decide if Yugoslavia or the Irish would progress. Despite all the possibilities, we did not have a rerun of the afternoon's non-action with both teams still giving their all. Less than quarter of an hour after the Irish euphoria, despair was cast over the nation. Mal Donaghy and Spain's Camacho sort of ran into each other on the touch line but the white shirted number 3 raised his hands and pushed out at his opponent. It was described as a fight by Motson. It is a good job he was never needed to call boxing, or he would have described David Haye's 2010 walkover (I refuse to call it a fight) over 'Fraudley' Harrison an all-time classic that should be revered by fans of the noble art in the same way as Hagler-Hearns and the Mickey Ward-Arturo Gatti trilogy. In the seventy-first minute Bingham replaced the attacking youngster Whiteside with his squad's most capped outfield player, defender Sammy Nelson, and the veteran helped his side hold on for a historic victory in the tensest game I had seen at this World Cup.

After the game, my dad, who had drunk a little too much Cointreau throughout the evening (I would love to tell you it was Guinness, but I never saw him touch the stuff), got out his reel-to-reel tape recorder and proceeded to play some Irish rebel songs, which he told me were illegal to own and that I had no idea he was in possession of. He had no IRA sympathies or to my knowledge had even crossed the Irish Sea but just appeared to like the tunes and the themes of rebellion. (I know these are from the southern side of the Irish border rather than the north but being a skinny teenager, I thought it wise not to point out the geographical error to my six-foot-two and full-of-booze father.) Anybody who ever knew him would confirm that he was not keen on authority or officialdom, whatever uniform it was wearing. Whilst we were both pleased the Irish had progressed by doing so as group winners, they had left England with an incredibly difficult task to reach the last four.

After the tournament's first rest days, the second group phase resumed. Each group consisted of three teams with the winners going through to the semi-finals. In an unusual format, but a decent one if you are going to have a second round of group games, any team that lost its first game would play in the next game against the group's yet untested third participant, meaning that each game would have something riding on it. As each group had all three of its games scheduled in one stadium (two based in Barcelona, the other two in Madrid) this did not cause any travel issues for fans or teams.

England against West Germany was the opening game of Group B, the last section to kick-off. England lined up with the team they had picked for the first two ties which meant no place for Glenn Hoddle in a team already missing Keegan and Brooking. In a theme that would become all too common over the years, England travelled to the finals with one or more of their star players carrying an injury, with no certainty of being fit enough to compete.

Second Group Stage

England lined up in their vibrant red shirts, which is my favourite England kit of all time, against the Germans wearing white, which was a repeat of the 1966 final. But that is where all similarities ended as the two teams played out a drab 0–0 draw which to my mind and many others was crying out for the vision and creativeness of Hoddle. Sadly, he stayed seated on the bench as firmly as any couch potato watching around the world. The singular change England made, in an era when managers often would not use their full complement of substitutes, was sending on Tony Woodcock with less than quarter of an hour remaining for fellow frontman Trevor Francis. This was the only group that opened with a draw so it was decided that Spain would play West Germany next, a game England hoped would produce another draw before facing the hosts in the section's final game. Many felt that Don Howe joining the England set-up in a coaching role had stifled Ron Greenwood's natural tendency to send his teams out to attack and on that night's evidence, they were right.

After each team had played at least once in the second stage four ties were left that, as intended, all had something riding on them. I still believed or at least hoped the final would be the game I had played out so often on my Subbuteo pitch, England versus Brazil. If not, there was still Northern Ireland to fall back on as long as they could complete the small task of defeating the French and being a Sunday afternoon, we settled down as a family to watch the Irish try to upset the odds once again. Midway through the first half, the possibility of an all-British semi-final came one step closer when Martin O'Neill sent his side in front, only for the goal to be cruelly and wrongly disallowed for offside. For the rest of the game,

I remember the French putting on a masterclass, taking a 4–0 lead, the same score they had beaten the Irish by in a friendly earlier in the year, before Gerry Armstrong scored a late consolation goal. Sunday of course meant party food in the non-party atmosphere, that had slightly improved from four years earlier, with the introduction of a choice of sandwiches— cheese and salad cream was now rustled up alongside the ham and tomato option that over the years had made more appearances than Peter Shilton, and sausage rolls had now forced their way onto our plates.

The next day, Mum picked me up from school for the final time during this World Cup. I arrived home in time for the first of two games that I was excited to watch, Brazil against Italy. The two teams had arrived with markedly different styles. Italy had drawn all their group games and only denied Cameroon the honour of being the first African nation to successfully navigate the group stages by the slimmest of margins. The Italians progressed from the incorrectly named Group 1. Of the six games only one was 'won', the other five finishing as draws, while the team managed by Frenchman Jean Vincent only had bothered the scoreboard on one occasion. Brazil, on the other hand, had come through the first stage with three victories and a goal difference of ten to two, with at least eight of their strikes filed in the draw marked 'top notch'.

In the second phase both Italy and Brazil had beaten defending champions Argentina, Italy by a score of 2–1 while Brazil took the points 3–1, a game in which Maradona was sent off near the end for a nasty balls high challenge on Batista in the same passage of play that the Brazilian had recklessly kicked Juan Barbas in the head. Whilst Maradona did not complain at seeing red, he claimed his intended victim was actually Falcao. As Argentina's number 10 bowed out of this World Cup, I had no idea of the effect he would have on the next.

Brazil only needed a draw to proceed to the next stage but, seemingly unable or unwillingly to settle for such a result, they, along with their opponents, treated the crowd that had packed into Espanyol's Sarria Stadium, along with millions of television viewers around the globe, to one of the greatest finals games ever witnessed.

Up front for the Italians that day was Paolo Rossi who had been banned for three years for his part in the 'Totonero' match-fixing scandal that saw him miss the 1980 European Championship finals on home soil.

The Italians scored only two goals in their four outings. His suspension was reduced to two years on appeal, which meant his firepower was welcomed back to the national team in a friendly against Switzerland just before the World Cup: coincidence or design?

The Italian number 20, who before this game had looked woefully off the pace required at international level, opened his Spanish World Cup account, along with the scoring that day, on five minutes. With just over a quarter of an hour left, the score was two-a-piece and Italy were awarded a corner that fell to Marco Tardelli on the edge of the box, who then sent his low shot goalward. Rossi reacted quickest to turn it past Peres in the Brazilian goal to complete his hat-trick and put the Italians into the lead for the third time that day. Brazil appealed for a non-existent offside and I, like all Brazilians, hoped that referee Klein would disallow the strike. But alas, he did not.

The match, one you would create if you delved into the dreams of young football fans around the world and amalgamated them, was not finished and still had more drama to give. Italy apparently scored a fourth that this time was disallowed for offside before Dino Zoff made a fantastic save preventing Brazil from drawing level once more. Italy held on to win 3–2 and booked an appointment with Poland on semi-final day.

Brazil going out disappointed the football fan in me but at the same time I knew this had made England's chances of winning the tournament that little more likely, but first, Spain stood in the way. In their previous outing the Spanish had been beaten 2–1 by the Germans, meaning that England needed to win by two clear goals to be sure of going through, while Spain had nothing to play for but pride. Being hosts meant they were not going to roll over in front of a packed Bernabéu in Madrid. As kick-off neared, I still had the optimism of somebody that had not yet seen his country fail at the World Cup and the side playing in white that night had ninety minutes to justify my faith. After all, Northern Ireland had beaten them, so why not England? The team news could have been better though; still no Keegan or Brooking in the starting line-up, as they joined the other player on the bench that I wanted to see on the pitch from the beginning, Glenn Hoddle.

The game had just passed the hour mark with no score when Greenwood played his final cards. Brooking with the unfamiliar number

3 on his back and Keegan with his favoured number 7 entered the fray; England had chosen the alphabetical route when assigning numbers but gave Keegan his traditional one.

Had the heroes of Budapest come to play less time than celebrity chef, Jamie Oliver, reckons it takes to whip up a tasty midweek meal or would they be the lightning rods that kept England's dream alive?

Brooking had a chance on the right forcing Arconada into a decent save, before the player who was more often than not selected as captain by Greenwood took centre stage. Bryan Robson magnificently created space for a cross from the left of the Spanish post before dinking a ball to Keegan in the centre of the goal. As the former European Footballer of the Year got his head to the ball it looked like England would still have twenty minutes to score a second, but somehow, he guided it wide and like Jack Charlton in the commentary box, I could not believe what I had seen. For the first time, it crossed my mind that England would not prevail and as the game finished 0–0, I had the joint feelings of despair and that somehow things were not quite fair. A feeling that I would become well acquainted with at regular four-year intervals.

Dad berated Greenwood for not bringing Keegan and Brooking on sooner in the game, and that turned out to be the thirty-one and thirty-three-year-olds' total experience of playing at a World Cup and the pair's last England caps. It was also the manager's last game at the helm for his country. Ron's twenty-two who had been lucky to be in Spain were equally as unlucky not to make the last four. They had won their original group at a canter, beaten one of the eventual semi-finalists (and had a better record than all the last four), were undefeated in their five outings, keeping four clean sheets whilst winning the only game in which they conceded, yet somehow, they were out.

And then there were four. After Italy had defeated Poland, another fantastic match was beamed around the world, one for me that surpassed even the Brazil-versus-Italy contest. France battling West Germany provided goals, drama, skill, thuggery and a little bit of history.

The Last Four

With England's exit, the World Cup was over as far as my parents were concerned and they had foolishly invited some friends over. For me though, it was not. I retreated to my bedroom and while I could hear laughter, the clinking of glasses and the sinking of pool balls, none of that could distract me from a classic clash.

The two teams exchanged goals in the first half an hour and the half-time whistle came far too quickly. Five minutes after the restart the French replaced the injured Geghini with Patrick Battiston who inside ten minutes was involved in one of the most horrific moments of any game.

The Frenchman ran onto a through ball from Platini and after sending his shot wide was poleaxed by a challenge from Germany's keeper Harold Schumacher inside the penalty area, in a move more akin to one you might see in a WWE wrestling ring rather than something that belongs between the white lines on a football field. A prone Battiston lost teeth, cracked ribs, damaged vertebrae, and was knocked out cold by Schumacher. After the Second World War, 110,000 Dutch citizens were punished for collaborating with the Germans and I am sure the French would have liked to see one more name added to that list when Dutch referee Charles Corver took no action against Schumacher. No penalty, no red card, no yellow, not even a free-kick.

A stricken Battiston was stretched off meaning that France had to use their second and final substitution while German coach Derwall still had two sets of fresh legs to throw on in the balmy Seville evening whenever he fancied.

The game finished 1–1 and extra time was required. In the ninety-second minute French centre-half MariusTresor scored with a centre-forward-like finish and six minutes later it looked like France would defeat one neighbour, when Alain Giresse put them 3–1 up, before facing another in the final.

The Germans though, were not yet done and in the final minutes scored twice to send the game to the World Cup's first ever penalty shoot-out. The French at this point did not know what England were destined to learn in the years to follow. The Germans are rather good in this situation.

Schumacher, who many believed should not have been on the pitch, saved two French penalties to send his team though 4–3 in the shoot-out. He had knocked France out twice on the same night.

So bad was his foul, at the final whistle I expected him to pick up a white

Persian cat before returning to a lair on some mysterious island where he would take charge of a criminal enterprise hell bent on world domination.

July 11 was the date set for the final and kick-off was an hour earlier than most of the evening games: 7:00 p.m. UK time. I had to decide who to support. Italy, who had done a number on Brazil with their forward who had been found guilty of match fixing, or the villainous Germans with cheater-in-chief Schumacher keeping nets? I chose the Italians, bribery being the lesser charge than assault. Paolo Rossi and Germany's Karl-Heinz Rummenigge stood alone in the race for the Golden Boot, tied on five goals apiece; if one could outscore the other they would win the individual reward.

Rossi struck first putting Italy 1–0 up before Tardelli and Altobelli gave the Azzurri an unassailable 3–0 lead. The Germans pulled a late goal back through Paul Breitner, who became the first non-Brazilian to score in two finals having also scored in the 1974 decider. The title was Italy's, the Golden Boot was Rossi's. What I remember the most from the night that Italy's forty-year-old captain Dino Zoff became the oldest player to win the World Cup is Tardelli's celebration. Nothing choreographed, nothing practised on the training ground, just sheer unadulterated, raw emotion as he ran from the scene screaming, clenching his fists, looking like he was going to run further than Forrest Gump on speed. I remember hearing years ago that he was shouting his own name. I am not sure if that is true, but I hope it is. If you wanted to sum up the emotion of football, that image did so perfectly.

Spain had wanted to show another side to the country after decades of Francoism and they did.

The games had been played in seventeen grounds across fourteen cities meaning that wherever you were on the mainland, a game would be played within a reasonable distance of you. But FIFA got lucky. When they had awarded the previous tournament to Argentina it was before the coup that put the country under the heel of a military dictatorship; however, when they selected Spain as hosts, they were still under the rule of General Franco. Fortunately for them and the Spanish people, he had died in 1975.

I am not sure what the optics of playing back-to-back tournaments under the foreboding shadows of dictators would have looked like.

MEXICO 1986

Big Jock's Ultimate Sacrifice

Of the three British nations that qualified for the 1982 finals, England had appointed Bobby Robson after Ron Greenwood's tenure came to an end. Ireland were still led by Bingham, who was hoping to become the first man from his country to appear at three World Cups, having been a player in Sweden in 1958, the last time the country had qualified before his stint as manager. Scotland had kept faith with Jock Stein.

England and Northern Ireland were drawn in a five-team group, meaning the top two teams would automatically qualify for Mexico, while Scotland were once again drawn with Wales, but being a four-team section, only the winners would automatically go through. The runners-up would have to negotiate a play-off to head to the home of tacos, tequila and tamales.

In November 1985, an already qualified England hosted an Irish side who knew a draw would be enough to see them through. A scoreless draw ensued which suited both sides. Bingham's men had qualified for consecutive tournaments for the first time in the country's history, whilst England stayed unbeaten in the group. However, a more memorable night had come a few weeks earlier when Wales hosted Scotland.

Going into Group 7's penultimate game, Scotland, Wales and Spain all had six points with one game each left to play. The Scots knew a victory meant Spain, when they faced Iceland in just over two weeks' time, would need a handsome win to deny them top spot, whilst a draw would guarantee at least a play-off berth thanks to their goal difference being superior to that of the Welsh. Wales knew they probably needed a victory to have any chance of qualification.

Stein, who was under immense pressure, had stopped taking his heart medication before the game so that he would not suffer any side effects and could concentrate clearly on the task at hand. In the build-up, people in the Scottish camp noted that he was not his normal self but put it down to the magnitude of the occasion. Scotland had lost the home tie to an Ian Rush goal and would have several players missing for the return due to injury or suspension, including skipper Graeme Souness.

Half-time arrived with the Welsh one goal to the good thanks to a Mark Hughes effort. Whilst Jimmy Greaves during his half-time ITV punditry suggested Jock Stein should be going berserk at his players for the goal conceded, the genial host could not have known how near yet how far his comments were from what Stein was doing in the dressing room. He was in the midst of a stand-up row with his number two Alex Ferguson about goalkeeper Jim Leighton who had looked shaky as the interval approached.

Jock screamed, "You never told me that Jim wore fucking contact lenses."

Leighton's club manager responded, "That's because I never fucking knew it myself," whilst teacups sailed through the air.

The veins on the temples of the two men were bulging to such a degree that if the confrontation had taken place in a Glasgow drinking establishment, the doormen would have left them to sort it out between themselves.

It turned out Leighton had worn contacts for years but had kept it quiet for fear of damaging his career, and who could blame him? Can you imagine the merciless chants from opposition fans at an actual short-sighted goalkeeper? On the other hand, what was unforgivable was not bringing a spare pair. So, the Mr Magoo of the goalkeeping world—see, that did not take long—was replaced by Alan Rough, who had not played a single game for his country since the defeat to Russia at the '82 finals.

Big Jock made his final managerial decision and one of the last he would make of any sort with around half an hour to play. He sent on Davie Cooper for Gordon Strachan and it was the substitute who levelled the score from the spot with less than ten minutes remaining on the clock. When Jock mistook the referee blowing for an infringement near the end of the game for the final whistle he stood, only to immediately collapse. He was rushed to the dressing room and Ferguson, conscious of Stein's words earlier to him about the importance of keeping your dignity, kept the players on the pitch, thanking the fans. As the cameras showed Stein being carried away from the pitch, commentator Brian Moore speculated that he had been overcome with emotion. If only that had been true.

When Ferguson made his way inside, he found Graeme Souness in tears and the player told him he believed 'The Big Man' had gone. He had. There was an immediate outpouring of love from players and fans alike with declarations that they would happily be out of the World Cup to have Jock still walking amongst them. Stein had some legacy. Not only had he crossed the sectarian divide and become Celtic's first ever Protestant manager, he had led the club to nine league titles in a row and was at the helm when they become not only the first British team but also the first non-Latin one to win the European Cup.

That evening, it was believed he had a heart attack but in fact he perished due to pulmonary oedema (fluid in the lungs) caused by heart disease, at the way-too-young age of 62.

Stein's funeral was held in quick order after the game and was attended by many famous faces including Rod Stewart, Lawrie McMenemy and Matt Busby, yet the world and the World Cup had to go on. It did so with Spain defeating Iceland 2–1 to top the group, confirming Scotland would need to negotiate a two-legged play-off against Australia to hear the words *"Bienvenido a Mexico"*.

The Oceania group winners travelled to Glasgow for the first leg but what chance did they have? Playing on an emotionally charged evening, the Scots not only had a twelfth man, thanks to the famous Hampden Roar provided by the sixty thousand-plus fans in attendance, they also had a thirteenth. Joining centre-half pairing of Willie Miller and Alex McLeish was the looming presence of 'Big Jock' himself, ensuring Scotland kept a clean sheet. Fittingly, Davie Cooper opened the scoring in a 2–0 victory.

This meant Ferguson, who had stepped into the breach, knew that his team could afford to lose by one goal and would still need to go searching through their drawers for their Spanish phrase books that had been gathering dust for the last four years, as they started the long and arduous journey to face off against their opponents who were trying to qualify for the first time since 1974.

The game in Melbourne finished 0–0 thanks to a strong display by Alan Rough. Scotland were going to their fourth finals in a row.

Colombia '86

On the last day of May the finals kicked off when champions, Italy, were held to a draw by Bulgaria in Mexico City on a Saturday night. I was now of an age when on weekends I was normally out in some bar or club, drenched in Denim aftershave, 'For men that don't have to try too hard'. More advertising baloney, as like most nineteen-year-olds, I had to try extremely hard just to have a conversation with a member of the opposite sex, let alone anything else. But then again, looking back, me and my oppos now remind me of *The Inbetweeners*, a coming of age sitcom about four teenage lads.

Although for the next few weekends that lifestyle was going to be curtailed somewhat, including for the opening match, a game that was staged around 2,000 miles north of where it should have been played.

Initially, Colombia was chosen as hosts in what was going to be a sixteen-team tournament that had expanded to twenty-four teams in Spain's World Cup before in 1982 the Colombians declared they could not afford to host such an event.

When the finals were awarded in 1974, the country was under the leadership of President Misael Borrero, but he left office the same year and without his guidance problems lay ahead. Belisario Betancur had come to power in 1982 and wasted little time in declaring "The 1986 World Football Championship will not be held in Colombia. We have a lot of things to do here and there is not enough time to attend to the extravagances of FIFA and its members."

In reality, successive Colombian governments had done little planning when it came to the necessary infrastructure to host such an event . He was right about one thing though, the country did have other things to concentrate on. It was a time when drug kingpin, Pablo Escobar, was inflicting terror and chaos in the country and had in fact that very year managed to get himself elected as an alternative representative to the Chamber of Representatives of Colombia's Congress. Known to be a huge soccer fan who built pitches for poor neighbourhoods, he was ruthless and unpredictable, so who knows what could have happened.

During the 1994 finals, whilst he was no longer walking amongst us, the Colombian drug cartels would make a statement that reverberated around the globe, but more of that later.

Brazil, Canada, the US and Mexico all offered to save the day. After the Brazilians quickly dropped out it was a three-horse race. Mexico was surprisingly chosen as hosts and although a football-mad nation, had staged the finals just sixteen years earlier.

At the time, because I learnt a lot of my geography about countries outside Europe or the Commonwealth thanks to football and because of Mexico's poor record at the finals, I assumed it was a small nation and not the massive one it actually was. The hosting duties were put to a vote, which Mexico won suspiciously easily and when it was discovered that Televisa were granted the broadcast rights, whose president was a close friend of FIFA supremo Joao Havelange, those north of the border who had harboured doubts about the validity of the process were outraged.

I had no clue about how things worked on the other side of the Atlantic at the time but now have a much stronger insight, for I moved to Mexico in 2015.

As I write this and look out of my office window at the house being built across the road, I watch builders wearing baseball caps instead of hard hats, using a ladder they have fashioned themselves from discarded bits of wood, perching themselves in the most improbable positions and I wonder how the country was ever ready in time for the World Cup. Especially after it experienced a devastating earthquake in 1985 that claimed thousands of lives and caused over four hundred buildings to collapse in the country's capital, where the two biggest of the twelve stadiums were located, but ready it was.

One thing that does not surprise me now is the controversy surrounding the winning bid. Mexico is a country where corruption is a way of life and money not only talks, it has a dialect all its own. For instance, many parents bring their children up with the shameful truth that, "Si no tranza, no avanza", which roughly translates as "If you don't scam you will not get anywhere in life". Another well-known phrase to anybody growing up in the country is "Piensa mal y acertaras" which means if you always start with the mind-set that something has been done wrong you will be proven right.

Naranjito (little orange), who was the mascot four years earlier, caused little or no offence. However, it was a different story when the figure that is always supposed to add a little fun to proceedings was revealed as Pique, with some in Mexico believing others would use it to have a little too much fun at their expense.

Pique was a green jalapeño pepper wearing a yellow sombrero who sported an outsized moustache and wore football boots that were so large any self-respecting clown would have thrown them in the bin. Some of the voices opposed to Pique expressed concerns that he had nothing to do with the Mexico of the time and that he was more like a 1930s Hollywood image of what a Mexican should look like and thought up by a bunch of *Gringos*, when in fact, it was designed by a Mexico City advertising firm.

One thing that did work was the name. In a country where virtually everything has a double meaning, Pique and its derivatives proved to be no exception. A spectacular player could be described as a "*picoso*". The straightforward PK is an abbreviated way of saying a penalty. In sporting terms if you get the better of your opponent you "*lo pico*" them or if you *picando* or *pisoneando* your adversaries you are taunting them, although these two can also have sexual implications. *Picante* is also the verb you use to describe something spicy.

A few things had changed for me personally. I had officially become a man the year before when I turned eighteen but had truly become one the year before that. We had moved house, about 200 yards. Dad had built a house on some land we owned and conveniently needed a labourer the year I left school, so I mucked in for six weeks before going to college and we then moved into our new, more modern accommodation in 1984. It had three bedrooms downstairs that led directly off the lounge, so I no longer had the prospect of anybody's face looming at a window and staring at me. I had also installed a decent-size colour television in my bedroom, which was a bonus, as several games were played at 11:00 p.m. UK time and with pubs not yet staying open that late, it meant I would not disturb my parents watching the late-night games. In fact, it was not just the late-night games, it was often the earlier games. As well as Dallas, Mum and Dad now were avid followers of a chatty Irishman by the name of Wogan and a programme that I believe has become the most depressing of all time—*EastEnders*.

Late Night Troubles

The 1986 World Cup was a vibrant, colourful affair that belonged to Platini, Butragueno, Laudrap and Lineker, but above all to one man, Diego Maradona. Whilst most of his contemporaries towered over him physically, in footballing terms it was he who would come to dwarf them.

My life was not as simple as four years earlier and I had commitments beyond getting myself to school and back in time for kick-off. As well as going to work in Rumbelows, the electrical wholesaler selling the colour TVs, microwaves and refrigerators that Dire Straits had sung about in their 1985 hit 'Money For Nothing', playing pool had become a big part of my life in the winter months, playing for different teams, four nights a week. Luckily in the summer, many of these leagues did not run and I only played one night a week but I also now regularly went to the gym, spent time with my mates and had my first proper girlfriend, although she disappeared during the tournament only to resurface with a friend of mine. For these reasons, along with the fact many of the games did not start until so late, watching as much live football as four years earlier was not a realistic prospect.

Happily, most of the Brazil, Northern Ireland and Scotland games were on in the 7:00 p.m. slot and the other team I took an interest in this time around was Argentina, mainly because of Maradona. All three of England's group games kicked off in the late slot so although this did not interfere with my social life, I am sure it affected my pay packet, as I probably did not pick up as much commission the days after England games. Although an inconvenience to the England fans back home, there was no real choice but to play the games in the late afternoon, as the midday heat during the summer months in the Monterrey area is stifling and it would just be impossible for a northern European team to play anywhere near its best.

England got off to a terrible start as I saw them beaten for the first time at a World Cup when they went down 1–0 to Portugal despite being the better side.

A few days before the game an open letter was printed in the English language paper *Mexico City News* from the three home nation's captains, Bryan Robson, Graeme Souness and Sammy McIlroy, urging the fans who were attending to stay in line. It came virtually a year to the day after the Heysel tragedy, where violence between Liverpool and Juventus fans led to a wall collapsing and the sad deaths of thirty-nine Italians. This had resulted in an indefinite ban on English clubs from European competition and nobody wanted to see the same thing happen on the international stage ever again.

Whether the letter worked, or it was only the genuine fans and not the troublemaking element that had made the long journey to Mexico, reports of trouble with British fans were few and far between. However, troubles for England were coming on the pitch.

Now while there is an old saying that nothing good happens after midnight, in England's match against Morocco everything went wrong shortly before Big Ben struck twelve. Just before the break, three things that would shape England's tournament happened in the blink of an eye. Firstly, Ray Wilkins picked up a yellow card. Then skipper, talisman and best player Bryan Robson went down and dislocated his shoulder, an injury the whole of England were fearful of as he had already suffered the same more than once playing for Manchester United and popped it out again in a warm-up game against Mexico in Los Angeles. Barely before Robbo had left the pitch in tears, he said as much in frustration and anger as the pain, Wilkins joined him when he lost his temper for possibly the only time in his career. Flagged for offside, he petulantly threw the ball at the Paraguayan referee who, chest out, thrust his right arm skyward as if he was a schoolboy desperate for the toilet. He brandished a red card, the first time any England player had received one at the finals. The country's captain and vice-captain were gone. Luckily, Morocco did not seem able or willing to press home their man advantage and the game finished scoreless. At least England had picked up their first point. How different everything felt to four years earlier.

Going for the Knockout

Going into their last games of the first stage, all three British teams still had a chance of progressing, thanks to another format change. This time, after the initial group phase, FIFA had decided the tournament should be played on a straight knockout basis, meaning the four best third-placed teams would squeak through along with the two best teams in each group to leave a final sixteen.

England were first up of the home nations and manager Bobby Robson made four changes. The first two enforced, Wilkins suspended and Robson injured, both of whom had played their last football of the tournament, were replaced by Steve Hodge and the best possible fill-in for Captain Fantastic, Peter Reid.

He also brought in Trevor Stevens for Chris Waddle, which diminished the chance for comedy value in our house. During one England game, possibly a qualifier as my parents had not stayed up for any of the late games, when the commentator announced, "Waddle across the pitch" my mum agreed, saying, "Yes, he does run funny."

However, the most telling change was bringing in Peter Beardsley for Mark Hateley.

This led to the first glimpses of late-night joy for England fans as Gary Lineker scored England's first goal of the tournament before also managing their second and third to complete a short-range first half hat-trick, as the Three Lions ran out 3–0 winners and into the knockout stages, claiming second place in Group F in which history was made. Not only did Morocco became the first African nation to make it out of the group stages, they did so by topping the section.

The next night it was Northern Ireland's turn, whose exploits in Mexico are retold in the very watchable *Shooting for Socrates* feature film. Now while everybody else had a regulation size squad of twenty-two, the Irish appeared to have added the radio and TV host I mentioned earlier, Terry Wogan, to theirs. What I mean by that is, the BBC only chose to show the second half of certain games for fear of disappointing the genial Irishman's audience by cancelling or daring to move his show.

Even with this twenty-third man, they found the might of Brazil too much, as they lost 3–0 and the Selecao were the first team through with maximum points.

The next day the Scots managed to become the last team knocked out in the initial stages after being given the easiest task yet to break their first-round hoodoo. In the very first minute against Uruguay, Jose Batista took out Gordon Strachan with such ferocity that he was shown a straight red card, the fastest in World Cup history. For the next eighty-nine minutes the South Americans carried on in the same vein, kicking the opposition nearly as often as the ball, but the Scots could find no way past and limped out of the competition literally and figuratively, thanks to a 0–0 draw. I remember Ian St John in the ITV studios being equal parts livid and disappointed.

After the game, La Celeste were fined for their behaviour, not just for that night, but their actions throughout the tournament. They also had had a player dismissed within twenty minutes against Denmark, who were proving to be one of the bright lights of the tournament and being tipped by many to win the whole thing, especially after they beat West Germany 2–0 to become only the second team through with three wins out of three.

One Bad Hombre

In the round of sixteen, England faced Paraguay and for the first time the English audience had the chance to watch their team in the early slot. So many in the country who had missed the pain of the group stage were only now getting their first live glimpse of Bobby Robson's men performing in Mexico. My dad, who was one of those, suggested we go to the pub directly across from our house called The Mount. When I was younger, we used to go sometimes as a family for a meal in the restaurant or to play pool, but this felt like my decision and I said I would rather watch it at home.

I had always had a bad feeling about the landlord, something just did not sit right.

Down the years he was accused of dealing in stolen paintings in Belgium, stealing grandfather clocks and being part of a heroin smuggling ring. The latter of these crimes, for which he served a prison sentence, albeit a shortened one because he turned Queen's evidence and became a 'supergrass', happened many years after the pub was gone and he had left the immediate area. However, his worst deeds were yet to come, something I could not have imagined. It was a few years later that he made headline news both in the UK and India. Kenneth Regan, or Avery as I knew him, had fallen on hard times since his drug smuggling days when he was known as 'Captain Cash' and craved the high life again, without caring how it came about.

He attempted to take over a Heathrow freight company owned by Indian businessman Amarjit Chohan. Unfortunately, this was no friendly takeover. Instead, Regan and his accomplices murdered not only Mr. Chohan but also his wife, his mother-in-law and most despicably of all, his two young sons aged just eighteen months and two months, all for financial gain. Regan is serving a whole of life sentence which is very rare in the UK, with estimates suggesting there are less than a hundred people currently in the prison system who have had that sentence imposed on them. Compare that to America where the number is believed to be more than fifty thousand. This puts him in extremely notorious company. Some other names you may recognise that had the same sentence handed down to them include Rosemary West, Peter Sutcliffe, Jeremy Bamber and Levi Bellfield. Chilling.

It meant we happily watched from the safety of our lounge as England defeated their opponents 3–0 thanks to a Peter Beardsley goal sandwiched between two more from Lineker. This was England's first experience of playing at over 2,000 metres above sea level. Paraguay had the advantage of playing their previous games at this raised height but watching the game you would never have known.

There was only one more game to play in the round of sixteen, Denmark taking on Spain, and when someone informed me the following day that it ended 5–1, I was not too shocked, until they pointed out that Spain were the victors thanks to a 'poker', a four goal haul from Emilio Butragueno.

I would see only two of the quarter-finals and Brazil against France meant a third Saturday night out of four at home indoors, but it was definitely a game worth staying in for.

In a mouth-watering clash it was Zico, Careca and Socrates taking on Giresse, Tigana and Platini.

Zico missed a penalty and the game ended 1–1 but it had an eerily similar passage of play to France's semi-final four years earlier. Striker Bruno Bellone was clear through on goal with only the keeper to beat when the Brazilian shot stopper made a cynical, but not this time brutal foul, to deny the Frenchman an almost certain goal. For some reason the referee waved play on and the two teams were going to have to settle their differences from 12 yards. God was definitely not French. In the ensuing penalty shoot-out Socrates and Platini both failed to convert their spot-kicks as the French were victorious 4–3. Had the French made a deal with the devil? This was one of three quarter-finals decided in this manner, with West Germany overcoming the hosts and Belgium getting the better of Spain the following night. However, before that tie there was the small matter of England taking on Argentina.

This was a clash with so much history already written it seemed inevitable that it would be added to.

In 1966 the two sides had faced each other at the same stage. Antonio Rattan, the South American's captain, was sent off in the first half for arguing with the German referee despite the two men not sharing a common tongue. Argentina's number 10, who to this day maintains that the referee was going to make sure England won under any circumstances, refused to leave the field for another eight minutes, apparently asking for an interpreter.

At full-time when the England players went to swap shirts with their opponents, manager Alf Ramsay ran onto the pitch to stop this from happening. After the game he labelled Rattan and his teammates 'animals', due to their style of play. Add to this that only four years earlier the two countries had been at war over the Falkland Islands, in a conflict in which far too many brave young men from both countries perished.

One more reason Argentina wanted to overcome the English was that they had introduced the beautiful game to them, so it was like the child finally beating the father and coming of age.

What's the saying: 'Only mad dogs and Englishmen go out in the midday sun'? Well, that day, eleven Englishmen, eleven Argentinians and a Tunisian referee, who would take centre stage, did just that along with over one hundred thousand spectators in Estadio Azteca. Even Maradona agreed with the above, suggesting that playing games at this time of day in the Mexican heat could cause somebody to die. While Argentina had an advantage in the fact that they had played all their games at over 2,000 metres above sea level, England had only played once at this altitude, their last match against Paraguay. When I have been in the nation's capital, I have not felt the altitude to be a problem but then again, the fact I was not playing football may have something to do with that. Also, several of my friends, be they Mexican or European, all say they feel it whenever they visit, including some that used to live there but have now moved away.

In the pre-match interviews, both sets of players said all the right things, that football had nothing to with 'Las Malvinas' and football and politics should not mix, but in reality it did, at least for Argentina. Maradona has since publicly stated that it was uppermost in his side's minds when they met.

Although I loved watching Maradona, I told anyone who would listen that there was only one way to stop him. The moment he got the ball he had to be fouled and the further away from the England goal the better. I did not mean anything brutal that would cause injury, just a shove or a barge that would disrupt his rhythm and I certainly was not advocating what one Venezuelan fan had done.

Maradona had not played for the national team between the last World Cup and the qualifying games for Mexico, not because of any dispute but purely because Carlos Bilardo was only selecting home grown players for the national side.

In Spain, Colonel Gaddafi lookalike Claudio Gentile playing for Italy had kicked Maradona from the first whistle to the last and Argentina's number 10 was fouled an unbelievable twenty-three times, a World Cup record for a single game. On his return to international football, the same treatment was awaiting him. This time before he had even arrived at the stadium.

Once the Argentinian squad had landed in San Cristobal, they could sense the crowd getting out of control and one of the Venezuelans broke through the police cordon and kicked Diego's right knee. Hard. He had injured Maradona's meniscus, but after a sleepless night with ice pressed firmly on the injury, the returning hero was passed fit to play. And he made Venezuela pay, scoring a brace, the first in the opening two minutes in a 3–2 victory. He played in all six of his team's qualifiers as they topped the four-team group. At the time, South America had three qualifying groups rather the one nine-team section they use now.

England centre-half Terry Fenwick certainly decided this was the way to deal with Argentina's captain, getting booked for a cynical foul on him inside ten minutes.

Half-time came and went with no score before the most memorable five minutes of international football of my life took place and I would venture of anybody's with English blood running through their veins.

Perhaps the only exception could be the 1966 victory, outside what we witnessed from Argentina's number 10 Diego Maradona.

England vs Argentina

Shortly after the restart, Maradona ran through the England defence and attempted to play a one-two with Jorge Valdano, but instead, Steve Hodge got to the ball first and played it towards his own goal. The 5-foot-5-inch Maradona outjumped the six-foot Peter Shilton in the England goal to head home. The England players immediately started to appeal, but I must admit I had not seen anything amiss and Barry Davies commentating for the BBC wrongly surmised the players were appealing for offside. In fact they had seen what Tunisian referee Ali Bin Nasser had missed. With a deft flick of his left hand, Argentina's star player had punched the ball into the net. As it became clear from the commentary that it was handball, I looked at my dad, a man slightly taller and broader than the England keeper and not somebody to be trifled with. He was staring intently at the television. I can only think he was imagining getting Maradona in a darkened room and 'having a chat'.

A few minutes later Maradona received the ball in his own half and then went on an incredible run that left England players in his wake much as Elvis Presley had done with Hollywood starlets. But unlike the young ladies who wanted an encore with the king of rock'n'roll, I doubt if anybody in the white of England wanted to see the architect of their downfall ever again. As he slotted the ball past a stranded Shilton, Davies declared, "You have to say that's magnificent." And he was right.

I stood and applauded for the simple reason that I had just witnessed the best goal I had ever seen, scored by greatest player to ever play the game, neither of which have in my opinion been surpassed to this day. A goal that is even better when you consider the state of the pitch it was scored on, a veritable ploughed field compared to the bowling green surfaces of today.

We were 2–0 down but still had over half an hour left and there was still time. I immediately started shouting for Bobby Robson to send on John Barnes, the Watford winger who a couple of years earlier had himself scored a wonder goal in the Maracaná against Brazil, another game that I recall only had the second half shown live. The England manager did indeed make a change but he put on the wrong wide man in my estimation, bringing on Chris Waddle for Peter Reid. Still no breakthrough and at last with just over quarter of an hour left Barnes was given his World Cup debut, his twenty-eighth appearance for his country. Within seven minutes he had made the difference I was hoping for. He got to the by-line and crossed for poacher supreme Lineker, who headed in his sixth goal of the World Cup. With the clock ticking down to full-time and Maradona still tormenting England he created a chance for Tapia who hit the post. Barnes again surged down Argentina's left flank and crossed for Lineker, who headed what looked to be the equaliser, and we were out of our seats celebrating. Somehow his effort went wide and instead of the ball, it was the Everton hitman that nestled in the back of the net.

That was it. England were out. The tournament's Golden Ball winner had defeated the Golden Boot winner. I can only imagine what a potent attacking force the two men who were born only a month apart would have made if they had ever been teammates instead of opponents.

The sublime talent that lit up the tournament or the short, fat little cheating Argie—if you have not got over that day—wrote in his autobiography that he took pleasure from both goals. He wrote that the one he christened the 'Hand of God' goal felt a little like pickpocketing the English. It is a goal many in Argentina will still defend to this day as inventive or mischievous. The English press unsurprisingly did not agree, with the headline in *The Sun* simply reading 'Diego The Cheat!'. While many members of the England team that day felt robbed of their chance at World Cup glory, he robbed me of something else, the chance to watch any more World Cup matches with my father. Like previous tournaments, once British representatives were out, he was out, so after seeing West Germany dispose of France in the semi-final in a repeat of four years earlier, I missed the late game when Maradona scored a sublime brace to knock out Belgium, leaving just the final.

I went over to my friend Mike Lodge's house and we sat and chatted as the game largely passed us by and Maradona inevitably had the last word in a match in which Lothar Matthaus had generally kept him quiet. Maradona provided a defence-splitting pass for Jorge Burruchage to score the last goal of the game, as Argentina prevailed 3–2 to claim the title for the second time. The tournament belonged to the man whose journey had taken him from Villa Foirito, a poor neighbourhood on the outskirts of Buenos Aires, to audiences with royalty.

I could not help but wonder how different things could have been if Bryan Robson had been fit for the quarter-final or if the referee had been fit for purpose. Could England have been crowned world champions?

Meeting Maradona

As I watched Maradona and his teammates celebrate their victory, little did I realise that thirty-two years later and less than 700 miles from the scene of his crime and greatest moment on a football field, our paths would cross.

In September 2018 Maradona was surprisingly named as the manager of Mexican second division side Dorados de Sinaloa. The speculation and jokes started immediately.

Anybody who has watched the Netflix series *Narcos Mexico* or *El Chapo* will be aware that Sinaloa is the birthplace of one of the country's most infamous drug lords Joaquin 'El Chapo' Guzman and is the home of the Sinaloa cartel. Due to Diego's well-publicised drug habit, Dorados quickly became known in Mexico as *Drogados*, meaning stoned or drugged in English. People also expressed the view that he had chosen to take this job as it would give him easy access to the white stuff whenever it took his fancy.

A few weeks into his reign, he took his charges to play against Venados in the beautiful colonial city of Merida which is about a three-and-a-half-hour drive from where I live. My stepdaughter was visiting from England and as she had never visited the state capital before, along with my girlfriend, we decided to go for a weekend break and take in the game. On match day, Maradona was bedecked in a pink bib that would have gone down a storm at a seven-year-old girl's princess party. The bib sat over the top of his eighties rapper outfit and he was the target of abusive chanting every time he ventured out of the dugout to encourage his team during the first half.

The game was quite dull and scoreless at the break; nevertheless we had the half-time entertainment to look forward to which included four scantily clad dancers, something commonplace in Mexico. I have seen them gyrating outside car accessory stores and builders' merchants at 11:00 a.m. The girls were accompanied by the home mascot, a horny stag (*venados* means deer in English) and at the same time the parade started; well, that's an exaggeration, it was three vans and two team mascots plus a random Bob the Builder.

Well, this nearly ended in disaster as things so often do here, when young Bob, who was so excited by his fifteen minutes of fame, tripped over his own outsized feet and hit the ground in a manner that put me in mind of Neymar on a windy day. The driver of one of the vans came within a yard of running the downed mascot over. I would have liked to see the insurance claim for that one. With disaster averted the second half got underway and Dorados scored the goal that put them into the play-offs.

At the final whistle, the man whose mere presence in the dugout had added an extra thousand on to the gate waved to the home fans and in an instant turned the jeers into cheers. I had just witnessed the Maradona effect first-hand.

After the game I was in the press area when he went to leave and he noticed the Art of Football t-shirt that I was wearing, which had been a birthday gift from a friend.

The design was him facing up to the Belgium defence in the '86 semi-final. He offered to sign it for me, so I said to him, "*Soy Inglés pero para mi siempre serás el número uno.*" (I am English but for me you will always be number one.) He chuckled and then was gone. Not in the fleet-footed manner of yesteryear but limping away as you would expect from a player than had been kicked on pitches all over the world by the world's best and worst defenders.

Many in England may still consider him a cheat but think how many times he was cheated against? He was frequently fouled, often brutally. I wish he had not scored that brace against England but at the same time, he surely is the player we all wish we could have been.

ITALY 1990

Moving On

By the time Italia '90 rolled around, my life had changed considerably. I had bought my first house aged twenty-one with Nick, a friend from college, but would still watch the whole of this World Cup back at my parents' house at Lopcombe Corner, a place so small it was often left off maps of the day, or if included at all, commonly misspelt as Lobscomce Corner.

Nick was a year older than me and although we attended the same secondary school, it was at college, whilst both enrolled on a BTEC Business Studies course, where we became friends. Double tax relief was coming to an end and with neither of us having a serious girlfriend at the time, well, not serious enough to buy a house with, we decided to club together. We were not the only ones to do this; another two sets of lads I knew did the same, all purchasing properties within half a mile of each other. Of the six, Nick was the only one who had not attended Winterslow Primary School, so I do not know if we had a teacher that had subtly extolled the virtues of home ownership, or that our own parents had encouraged us.

England had qualified for their third World Cup in a row, this time as runners-up to Sweden in their group, with a fantastic defensive record. They had played six qualifiers but had not let in a single goal. Scotland had qualified amazingly for their fifth tournament in a row. To give that some context, they have only played in one of the seven finals held since.

In qualifying, Northern Ireland were drawn in a five-team group that included familiar foes Spain and neighbours, the Republic of Ireland. The Spanish topped the group and Ireland, led by Englishman and 1966 World Cup winner, Jack Charlton, qualified for their first ever finals. Also making their bows at this level were Costa Rica and the United Arab Emirates. Missing were the hosts from four years earlier, disqualified during the qualifying process due to the Cachirules scandal (Cachirul is a

Mexican slang word that means fake or cheat) in which they knowingly fielded over-aged players in the 1988 CONCACAF Under-20 tournament.

I was now working as a financial advisor for Sun Life of Canada which meant I had a lot of freedom to plan my own schedule. Inevitably this involved a lot of evening appointments and I also had a second job as a nightclub doorman.

My parents had decided to go to the United States for six weeks and had asked me to look after their house, so I stayed there for the whole time they were away. That worked well with my security commitments as it took about a quarter off my journey time, as I was working in Basingstoke most Friday and Saturday evenings.

While I remember Mexico because of Maradona, my memories of Italia '90 are moulded by the genius of a twenty-three-year-old Geordie scamp, a fifty-four-year-old Italian opera singer and the games and minutes I missed as much as the ones I saw.

The opening game between champions Argentina and Cameroon was on a Friday evening at 5:00 p.m. The powers that be at ITV appeared to have forgiven the South Americans for their part in the Falklands War and unlike eight years earlier, happily broadcast the game. History was to repeat itself as the reigning champions again would go down 1–0. With the game goalless at just past the hour mark, Andre Kana- Biyik of Cameroon received a red card, the first of sixteen during the finals, for a foul on Claudio Caniggia. While Andre may have brought shame on the family name, six minutes later his brother Francois had righted that wrong when his tame header somehow squirmed past Argentinian shot stopper Nery Pumpido, whose goalkeeping some may compare to Sunday league but to me it looked more like a chess player had been given the gloves and been told to do his best. It was hard to imagine that he was going to pick up a second winner's medal if he kept that form up.

With less than five minutes to go Caniggia forcefully broke forward again before one, then a second, and then a third African player tried to end his run, not caring whether their challenges were within the rules, in a passage of play that looked like a brutal game of Pac-Man. The final culprit Benjamin Massing received his marching orders, yet at the full-time whistle it was the side with only nine men left that were celebrating a surprise victory.

The next night when I would have been at work, Salvatore 'Toto' Schillaci started to make the tournament his own. The twenty-five-year-old Juventus striker had made only one appearance for the Azzurri before being selected in the Italian squad, hoping to emulate the team of 1934 by capturing the trophy on home soil. With the game tied at 0–0, Toto, the common Italian nickname for anybody christened Salvatore, was given fifteen minutes to show what he could do but only needed three to make his mark, scoring the game's only goal with a close-range header.

With Mum and Dad being away, my three closest friends at the time, Bill, Simon and Lodgey (another Mike), spent a lot of time at the house, sometimes joined by our neighbour Biffa, who had bought our old house, and a few other occasional interlopers such as Martin Bray. We had several BBQs, the first for the Brazil versus Sweden game that the South Americans won. It was a game that began a little bit of unwanted history for their opponents. They became the first team to play three games at a World Cup and have them all finish with an identical result—a 2–1 defeat.

A Flair for the Dramatic

Now, while South American qualifiers were not shown on British television at the time, one game that became known as 'El Marcanazo' did make it onto the news, and if Chilean goalkeeper Roberto Rojas' sharp tactics had worked, Brazil's proud record of appearing at every finals could have come to a halt with their appearance in 1986.

The two sides were placed in a three-team group with Venezuela, a team they both took maximum points from, so it was a straight shoot-out between the two combatants for the one qualifying berth. The first clash in Chile that finished a 1–1 draw was such a bad-tempered affair that both teams were reduced to ten men in the opening minutes and Chile were ordered to play their next 'home' qualifier in Argentina.

The game's last section saw Chile needing a victory in the Maracaná while the Brazilians knew a draw would suffice.

Early in the second half, Careca gave Brazil the lead to pretty much seal the deal, but then halfway through the second period the incident that would cause mayhem occurred.

A flare was hurled onto the pitch, landing about a yard from the Chilean goalkeeper. For a player who had spent his whole career in South America, the sight of a flare landing on the pitch was nothing new, but the stopper immediately fell to the ground and was surrounded by concerned teammates. In fact, so concerned were they that they decided not to wait for a stretcher to remove the stricken goalie from the pitch but to carry him themselves with blood seeping from a cut. With their first choice keeper unable to play on, a medical certificate was duly produced by the team doctor. Chile declined to return and finish the game. Such crowd disorder can have serious consequences for participating teams. There was a real possibility that Brazil could be docked points or even kicked out of the tournament.

The culprit who had thrown the flare onto the pitch was quickly discovered to be twenty-four-year-old Rosemary Mello de Nascimento, who was detained by the police.

However, it soon became clear that although the flare landed close to Rojas, it had not hit him or caused harm in any way, confirming the suspicions of several of the Brazilian team. It transpired that amongst the melee, he used a razor he had secreted in one of his gloves, as all the world's best keepers do to this day, I am sure, and the wound was in fact caused by Rojas himself wielding the blade.

Once the constabulary realised that Rosemary's actions had not caused the abandonment of the game, she was free to go and much like the trajectory of her missile, her career took off. She became a celebrity who would become known as *Fogueteira de Maracaná* (Firecracker of Maracaná) and in a country where overt sexiness wanders down every street on an hourly basis, even adorned the cover of *Playboy* magazine.

FIFA handed out bans like Sven Goran Erickson did caps in friendlies, including a lifetime playing ban to Rojas (which got overturned in 2001) and Brazil were awarded the game 2–0 to confirm their place in Italy. Chile was effectively disqualified along with the Mexicans for their game of 'hide the birth certificates'. To further rub salt into the self-inflicted wound, Chile were banned from the 1994 World Cup.

In 2014 Brazil hosted the finals but sadly Rosemary would not be around to light up the crowd; she passed away at just forty-five years old due to a brain aneurysm in 2011.

England Lucky to B Seeded

England were the sixth and last seeds and this again brought rumblings of discontent. The Dutch and Spanish argued that this spot should go to them, as England had only been awarded this on-field advantage so that the authorities could ensure the Three Lions were placed in Group F and based on the islands of Sicily and Sardinia. It would make it easier to control the hooligan element that dogged the English game at the time, rather than being on the mainland, especially with Italy being a lot closer and more affordable to travel to than Mexico. This proved to be a wise decision as far more of the troublemaking element arrived on Sardinia where England would play all three of their group games.

The argument from the Dutch became null and void when they were drawn in England's group along with Egypt and the Republic of Ireland.

England's first opponents were the Irish who were rather disparagingly called the England 'B' team thanks to the way Jack Charlton implemented the grandparent rule, which meant you could play for the land of your parents or grandparents.

He took extreme advantage of the law. It seemed if you were a decent player and your grass was the same shade of green as the Irish team jersey or if you had been to Dublin on a stag weekend, you had a chance of making the squad. However, while reports that the purchase of an Irish Wolfhound would automatically put you under consideration proved wide of the mark, over half the squad were born outside the Emerald Isle.

Bill and Lodgey joined me for most of the England games, and I believe Simon did for one or two. Although none of them were football fans, the World Cup worked its magic like it does on people around the globe every time it comes round and turned them, like many in the country, into England supporters for at least the duration of the tournament. That was helped by the timing of the games, much more viewer friendly 4:00 p.m. and 8:00 p.m. slots in the UK.

After missing Scotland being beaten by Costa Rica, this time I would only see one of their games. We settled down to watch England and the Irish play out a 1–1 draw in a group where five out of the six matches would end all square.

Not Witnessing a Camel Break Its Leg

Along with the BBQs and glorious weather, two of my clearest memories of Italia '90 are related to games I missed plus a missing five-minute spell of one I saw.

Argentina's second game was an 8:00 p.m. kick-off against the Soviet Union and my last appointment of the day was at the same time in Winchester with an 'orphan'. This was the name given to a customer if the rep who had signed them up had left the company and they were reassigned to those of us still there at the time. Usually when we went to see these customers, the appointment rarely lasted more than thirty minutes.

With Winchester being around a twenty-minute drive from Lopcombe Corner I figured I would be back home in time to see the start of the second half. How wrong was I?

The product that this customer had, let us call him Julian, was a pension. I went through all the normal questions: Are you happy with the product? Are the payments affordable? Do you see your circumstances changing soon? I got all the usual answers and there was nothing out of the ordinary, which led me to believe that he would just happily carry on paying the premiums until his chosen retirement age many years into the future.

Once we finished up, I asked if I could borrow his house landline—mobile phones were still a few years away for most people—to ring Mike who was going to pick up fish and chips and bring them over. "Of course," came the reply, and although Julian stood suspiciously close to me, I thought nothing of it. The family phone in Mike's house was engaged and it was at this point I made my fatal error. I had put my briefcase on the table and Julian, who could hear the engaged tone said, "Try again in a few minutes" and then informed me he was studying Jehovah and wanted to tell me all about it. Whilst I was still processing what this meant, I naively thought he meant some evening course he was taking; with the deftness of Roberto Baggio he had trapped my briefcase under some pamphlets. It slowly dawned on me that he was a Jehovah's Witness. Now while I had always been told not to let them in the house unless I wanted to listen to their spiel, nobody had ever thought to tell me what I should do if I found myself trapped in one of theirs, as they ramped up the rhetoric.

Well, of course, every time I tried Mike's house the phone was engaged. I found out later it was his sister hogging it when I really needed to use a lifeline. This meant Julian was in his element, telling me of the impending end of the world. I remained polite for as long as I could, all the while thinking that if it went on much longer, I may help Julian out and get him one step closer to God. However, I felt there was one question I must ask.

"If you believe the world is coming to an end, why have you got a pension that does not come to fruition for another twenty-five years?"

"Yes, I was thinking of cancelling it," came the galling reply.

I thought, *Really? You could have told me that when I arrived and we could have both gotten on with our lives.*

I finally got home after Argentina had defeated the Soviets in a game where their keeper Pumpido broke his leg and I would have gladly swapped places with the player known as 'The Camel' in Argentina—I have no idea where that moniker came from, but I certainly had the hump—instead of having to listen to a doom merchant tell me the end is nigh!

Twelve and Out

June 16 fell on a Saturday, meaning the England game that night was the first one I missed of the twelve they had taken part in since I had started watching the World Cup. I was working at Martines nightclub. Now normally I really enjoyed being at Martines; we floated between several locations that the boss Priestly provided security for and this was my favourite. However, I wanted to be at home to see the game. I managed to listen to the first half on the radio during the drive to work.

One of the other doormen was CJ who was related to the British boxer Lloyd Honeyghan, a man who had pulled off one of boxing's biggest upsets when he travelled to Atlantic City and defeated the hitherto unbeaten Donald Curry to become the undisputed welterweight champion of the world.

Around this time British boxing was on the up and up thanks to fighters of the quality or everyman appeal of Nigel Benn, Michael Watson, Chris Eubank, Frank Bruno and Lennox Lewis, with their bouts often being shown on terrestrial television. On those nights CJ would bring in his portable television. Now this worked well for boxing because we would shut the front door for each round and then let a few punters in as the fighters took their minute rest between stanzas and the management never really minded, as this made the club look busier than it was and we Brits seem to love a queue.

While I hoped CJ had brought his set with him for the England game, deep down I knew he would not as it was never going to be practical to keep the customers stood outside for forty-five minutes. As it turned out we could have done so because only a few waifs and strays turned up while England were battling the Dutch.

It must have been just before ten when, for argument's sake, let's call him Richard, strolled up and proceeded to tell us England had won 1–0 thanks to a Stuart Pearce free-kick right at the death. Okay, I had missed the game but at least we had won and now we were in a strong position to claim the group. Smiles all round and as we were always allowed a few guests of our own, and I had none booked in that night, I told him to go in for free as thanks for delivering the good news.

Fifteen or so minutes later, a group of lads showed up looking as sad as an Irishman halfway through a course of antibiotics on St. Patrick's Day. I greeted them with "What's up, lads, we won?"

"No, we didn't, it was a draw, 0–0."

"But Psycho's free-kick won it for us."

"It was disallowed."

Hmm, maybe they were winding us up. We waited for the next group to come in and after a very similar discussion I knew what I needed to do. I went and found my new 'friend' and told him I needed a word, The music was too loud to talk and I told him to come back to the front door, which he did without hesitation. Why wouldn't he? I was the kind doorman that had let him in for free.

We stepped outside and I explained to him what I had been told and it turned out the moment the free-kick hit the back of the net he left and was unaware it was disallowed.

I explained as calmly as I could that this was no real excuse. It was time for him to leave early again. Understandably he was not impressed and I saw the glint in his eye as he was about to go all John Wayne on me. I stared Dick in the face and told him he could either leave now and come back in next week with no issues or he could argue with me and cop a month's ban, and that for every word, every single word he uttered, another week would be added. Luckily, he saw sense and toddled off. In Basingstoke at the time, it was quite a big deal if you got knocked back from Martines as there was only one other nightspot to go to and that was an expensive taxi ride away.

Abuse of power, overstepping the mark? Maybe. But you should never leave a game before the end. I bet he never made that mistake again.

Flying Through or Home?

Come their last game, as always, Scotland had a chance of progressing but being up against Brazil, expectations were lower than previous tournaments. However, with the format being the same, if they could secure three points from their three games, this would give them a strong chance of going through as one of the best third-placed teams. Having beaten Sweden in their second game, a draw would suffice. They so nearly held out, conceding the only goal of the game with less than ten minutes to play to confirm that once again 'the knockout stages' would not need translating into Scots, the indigenous language of the land. It seemed however hard FIFA tried to help Scotland make it through to the second stage, the team tried just as hard to torture their fans with false hope before predictable failure.

The next night saw the final teams through to the knockout stages with England taking on the Egyptians at the same the Irish were facing the Dutch and with all four teams sat on two points and exactly the same goals for and conceded, they all still harboured hopes of progressing and possibly winning the group. One slip also meant they could finish bottom of the section. Unfortunately, lightning had struck twice when once again skipper Robson picked up an injury against Holland. It would rule him out of the entire tournament. Unlike four years earlier when he had stayed around in the possible hope of playing again, his Achilles tendon injury saw Alex Ferguson send him back to Manchester post haste.

On a nervy night, England won 1–0 thanks to a Mark Wright header and Lodgey had discovered a new game. Paul Parker had come into the team against the Netherlands and kept his place, so every time the commentator said "Parker", "Yes, m'lady?", as in *Thunderbirds*, quickly followed.

This slim victory meant England topped the section as the night's other game ended in a 1–1 draw, when a Dutch side containing Ronald Koeman, Rudd Gullit and Marco van Basten was held by a team containing Chris Morris and Mick McCarthy, whose most infamous World Cup moment would come twelve years later. This result meant that both sides ended up dead level leading to the drawing of lots to decide their final group positions. The Irish won this battle but as Holland were one of the best third-placed teams, they also progressed. I cannot imagine what it would be like to see your team knocked out in this fashion.

The tournament played against the beautiful backdrop of cities such as Rome, Florence and Verona had failed to live up to the previous ones on the pitch but with the sudden-death phase on the horizon everybody hoped this would all change. Alas, it did not.

Of the sixteen games left, only twice did teams score more than two goals. Compare that with 1994 when it happened on six occasions and 1998 (five) from the same number of games.

Instead, there was spectacle in the crowd as Cameroon, who had topped their section, opened up this stage of the tournament against Colombia who had support in the stands from 'The Birdman of Colombia'. Gustav Llanos would be held by his buddies from a rope and precariously dangled from one of the stands, bedecked in his resplendent red, yellow and blue condor costume, flapping around like an Italian traffic policeman in Naples on match day.

While Colombia had scraped through in third place in their section, they nearly had to scrape the brave but slightly insane Gustav off the concrete.

In their previous game when Freddie Rincón netted an injury time equaliser against Germany, his buddies forgot themselves, and more importantly, Gustav. In a moment of celebration that I am sure we can all empathise with, they let go of the rope, meaning he had about two seconds to really learn to fly. Luckily one of his friends had been forward thinking enough to tie the rope around his waist and disaster was averted.

Yet calamity could not be averted for Los Cafeteros. Already one down from a Roger Milla strike, Rene Higuita in the Colombian goal decided that rather than just clear his lines when he was a good 10 yards outside his area with the ball at his feet and a Cameroonian hitman bearing down on him, he would try to beat him. Well, that went as well as expected and Milla dispossessed him before rolling the ball into an empty net and running to the corner flag to celebrate in his now familiar fashion.

Higuita was certainly not averse to taking chances; he spent time hanging out with Pablo Escobar. I very rarely criticise individuals taking on players in the hope of making something happen. I do draw the line at the keeper trying to be Maradona, who the next day would set up Caniggia to score the only goal of the game, as they sent their biggest adversaries, Brazil, home.

On a day of footballing rivalries, we fired up the BBQ before that evening's entertainment when the Germans took on the Netherlands, two teams and two sets of supporters that again did not care for each other, in a game that took a turn that nobody saw coming and one that would certainly put you off your food.

The Ultimate Spat

Part of the charm of the World Cup is watching an underdog triumph whether by skill, determination, luck or a combination of all three, but also seeing two of the big guns go at each other, especially in the latter stages.

Netherlands, the European champions, taking on West Germany was such an occasion. A game to be anticipated and did not disappoint, but it is overshadowed by an incident in the first half that is thankfully a rare occurrence on the football field.

At the time, Italian football was the place to see and be seen and when the two sides lined up for kick-off at Milan's San Siro, six of the combatants played their home club football at the stadium. It was shared then as it is now—by Milan and Inter. Just to make sure harmony had no chance of breaking out, they were neatly divided down the middle by club as well as country. The three Germans were Internazionale players while the Dutch contingent all collected their wages from Milan.

With just over twenty minutes played, Frank Rijkaard fouled Rudi Voeller and then spat at the back of the German's head, who was understandably incensed and started arguing with his Dutch counterpart as both players were booked. I remember Bill jumping to his feet and pointing at the television whilst repeating, "He spat at him, he spat at him." I assured him that it was a rare occurrence on the football field. Almost immediately a hyped-up Voeller went in on the Dutch keeper with a challenge that looked like a foul and a dive at the same time and his new best mate was on the scene immediately to remonstrate with him and they both saw red. As they were walking off the pitch with Voeller a step ahead, Rijkaard did it again, an almighty gob at the back of the German forward's head. Many games are spoiled by a red card but this was not one of them, with Jurgen Klinsmann treating us to one of the World Cup's all-time best individual performances in a 2–1 victory. I have no idea if Rudi ever appeared in an advert for a shampoo company but if he did not, a trick was surely missed.

Over the next two days, Ireland and then England entered the sudden death stage of the tournament. The Irish played out a 0–0 draw with Romania and after thirty minutes of extra time failed to break the deadlock. Spot-kicks were needed. The first eight were all converted before Packie Bonner denied Romania's penalty taker. The question now was who would take Ireland's fifth, one that could send them to the last eight in their first ever finals?

I can only imagine what was being said in living rooms throughout Southern Ireland and going through Jack Charlton's mind—he had just let the players sort out who was going to take the spot-kicks—when centre-half David O'Leary emerged from the Irish ranks. A left-foot shot sent the Romanian keeper the wrong way and Ireland on to a quarter-final clash with Italy in Rome.

However, this did cause a problem for Big Jack. One of his back-room staff had asked the manager if they got to Rome would they get to meet the Pope? Jack had said yes.

Did he think they would not get there or was he just placating him like you might a small child that asks too many questions? Only Jack himself knows but somehow, they did get to meet the pontiff. After being introduced, the Pope did a blessing and with it being translated into several languages, it went on for longer than Ireland's match with Romania and Jack sadly fell asleep. He woke up in time to see the Pope waving to him; he waved back only to realise it was just a general wave not one specifically aimed in his direction!

The next night England were taking on Belgium and another 0–0. For the first time since 1970, an England game would need extra time. Just as everybody started to ready themselves for penalties, Paul Gasciogne went on a surging run that drew a foul inside the opponent's half. He floated the subsequent free-kick into the box and David Platt with a superb spinning volley scored the winner. Queue wild celebrations in our living room and across the country. People were starting to fall back in love with football and managing to see that the hooligans did not and never would represent the true fans.

The first three quarter-finals only produced two goals as Argentina, Italy and Germany made it to the last four.

We've (Not) Got the Power

England versus Cameroon would supply the last semi-finalist. English supporters, press and the team itself were supremely confident, although Cameroon had beaten reigning World champions Argentina, won their group and had super-sub Roger Milla amongst their ranks. Despite all these warning signs, it was still felt that losing to an African side would have been an embarrassment, especially as their opponents were missing three or four of their favoured starters. The confidence did not seem misplaced when Platt gave England the lead inside the opening half an hour.

Around the hour mark Cameroon were attacking and just at the precise moment England gave away a penalty, just about the worst thing that can happen when you are watching your country in a World Cup quarter-final happened—the electricity went off. Living where we did during the seventies and eighties, power cuts were common but becoming less frequent. After looking out and seeing the neighbours still had lights, I presumed it must just be the trip switch, but the question was, where was the fuse box? I did not actually know and nor did any of the others. Being in the middle of nowhere, there were no streetlights, so once we had found a torch, me and Lodgey searched, while the others made unfunny jokes. We started in the kitchen and found a hole at the back of a cupboard going through to a bedroom.

It was there, hiding behind some shirts on hangers, that we eventually found the misbehaving fuse box. A flick of the switch, power was restored and we were back to watching England. The question now was would it be 1–1 or would Shilton have saved the penalty? We were more than a little surprised to find the score was now in fact 2–1 to Cameroon. The only good thing was, we had not suffered, well, at least not live, that horrible feeling when somebody scores against your nation at a World Cup.

In the last ten minutes Lineker won, then converted a penalty before repeating the trick in extra time to send the Three Lions through.

In the first semi-final Italy went out on penalties to Argentina thanks to two saves in the shoot-out by La Albiceleste stand-in goalkeeper Goycochea.

Wednesday July 4 was the date set for the biggest game of football I had ever seen my country play, the World Cup semi-final. If we could beat probably our biggest footballing rival and a country we had been at war with forty-five years ago, we would face the team that had over the years become our second biggest rivals, a country we had been at war with far more recently and one that had denied England possible footballing glory four years earlier.

This was going to be a hard game. Germany had looked the team of the tournament so far and many believed whoever won tonight would become champions four days later.

Gazza's Tears

'World in Motion' was the official England song for the tournament, recorded by New Order and about half a dozen of the squad. It included the famous rap by John Barnes and when Gazza accepted a gold disc for the record that topped the UK chart on the afternoon of the game, he had no idea of the drama that would unfold that evening in Turin.

The BBC, in a master stroke, had chosen Nessum Dorma by Pavarotti as their theme tune and the smooth Des Lynman, one of the few men a moustache did suit, promised us at the beginning of the tournament that we would be humming it, and he was right. Anybody who watched that World Cup in England is instantly transported back to Italia '90, when they hear the song that appeared to have been written specifically for that night. The drama kept coming and coming and built and built to its amazing crescendo just as the song does, one that finishes with Vincero—I will win, nearly Luciano, nearly. It is so recognisable and so associated with that summer, it takes me back as quickly as I would leave the sea if I heard the theme tune from *Jaws*. In fact, if I heard that piece of music when I was in the bath, I would probably get out!

In a tight game, it was Germany who would draw first blood on the hour mark. Andreas Brehme sent his free-kick towards the England goal and Paul Parker tried to close him down, only for the ball to spin off of him and loop over Shilton's head, who clutched desperately at thin air, suddenly looking every bit his age. Beardsley, Gazza, Lineker, Walker and Platt looked on helplessly like a family of depressed meerkats.

England had gone behind in a cruel fashion and had half an hour to save their and a nation's dream.

I was still confident, especially when you look at that team. It was full of really strong characters and although well rewarded, this was the last England side in my opinion that appeared to care just as much as the fan in the street. Now I am not saying modern players don't care, you could not get to the top if you don't. There are always individual cases such as David Beckham, but how many recent England players since the turn of the century could match people such as Stuart Pearce, Terry Butcher and even the quieter ones like Lineker for sheer determination, character and togetherness? The only time I think I have believed England could possibly reach a final since then was 1998 under Glenn Hoddle, when ironically, Beckham received his marching orders in the game that confirmed I was wrong.

Parker was devastated and went missing, only rejoining the land of the living after providing the cross for Lineker to equalise with ten minutes left. Into extra time we went and in the ninety-eighth minute Gazza, whilst battling for the ball, overreached and fouled Thomas Berthold who rolled around as if he was the love child of Luis Suarez and Neymar. Gazza saw yellow; we saw his bottom lip start to tremble and Lineker telling the bench, and it felt like all of us at home, to keep an eye on the side's lightning-rod. It was his second booking of the tournament meaning he would miss the final if England got through. It was a yellow card that would affect a nation in so many ways.

There was still time for both sides to hit the woodwork, Chris Waddle's effort looking like it was in all the way until it hit the inside of the post and rebounded agonisingly out of David Platt's reach.

The game would need to be decided by spot-kicks. I had seen other teams have to deal with the pressure and emotions that brings but never an England side. Little did I know how many times over the years I would have to suffer this most entertaining yet horrible, despicable way to decide a match whilst supporting my country.

England's first three penalty takers were Lineker, Beardsley and Platt and each time they stepped up, I told the lads they would score and I was right. Unfortunately so did the Germans. This is where I was not so confident, although without Shilton, I don't believe we would have gotten as far as we did. The at-the-time record England cap holder went the right way each time but as he flung his ageing frame across the goal, he increasingly looked like the forty-year-old bloke that was still nightclubbing and every time he thought a twenty-three-year-old girl was within his grasp, she would move away at the last moment.

Stuart 'Psycho' Pearce walked forward. I distinctly remember somebody saying, "But he's a defender." I calmly explained he was going to score, as he took the penalties for his club side and had more bottle than the milk marketing board. I do not know what happened, but I do know Illgner in the German goal saved it. Once Olaf Thon had put West Germany 4–3 up, the next player who stepped up for England had to score or it was all over. Gazza had not been able to contain himself and was in floods of tears, meaning he was in no fit state to try his luck. England needed a replacement and that turned out to be his fellow Geordie Chris Waddle. I remember thinking instantly we are out. For me, his end product was never good enough. The others looked at me, but I could not say what I felt and he blazed his effort over the bar, meaning Germany and not England were needed in Rome four days later.

The England left-back was also unable to hold back the waterworks and the country fell back in love with the beautiful game thanks to the team's personality allied with their willingness to never give up, as well as the tears of a clown and those of a player know as Psycho. People could identify with these highly capable but fallible guys. The casual fans that had tuned in suddenly realised the majority of English fans were decent people. It was a small minority dragging their knuckles and the English flag through the mud.

England played their first ever third-place play-off and I had the night off. Priestly, like a good manager, rotated his squad so every five or six weeks you got a break. We had a bit of a party which seemed appropriate, as the Three Lions presented the hosts with a couple of gifts in a 2–1 defeat, the winner being netted by Schillaci from the spot to give him the Golden Boot. A man with eyes so expressive, you knew what he was thinking before he had fully formed the thought.

Sunday was the final in which I wanted the Germans to win. The others decided to give it a miss and as in the opening game, I saw two red cards in a 1–0 defeat for Argentina, thanks to a Brehme spot-kick. In the eight games from the quarter-finals onwards, fifteen goals were scored, six from the spot, but not the ones that mattered the most for England. The team that lost the shoot-out with a mere thirty million of their compatriots watching on.

Many of this England team had travelled to Mexico four years earlier and felt robbed of the chance at glory by Maradona, but he stole something else from me. My parents came home a few days after the final and within three weeks, my dad had died in Salisbury hospital. This meant I would never have the chance to watch football again with my hero. The last time we had done that, Maradona had punched the ball into the net and at that time, it felt like he had done the same to my heart.

USA 1994

A Qualified Failure

USA 1994 was the first World Cup held in an English-speaking country since 1966; well, nearly. As the famous quote goes, 'England and America are countries separated by a common language'.

For the first time I saw the tournament held in a third world country, not in real terms, but definitely footballing ones. Although that is not the story now, thanks in large part to the amazing success of the United States women's national soccer team. If you are in any doubt of how things were at the time, just watch the opening minutes of *Two Billion Hearts*, FIFA's official film of the tournament.

Bobby Robson's last game as England boss was defeat to Germany at Italia '90. After the run to the last four that included hard proof that Paul Gascoigne could deliver on the biggest stage and looking ahead four years, hopes were high that England could go one better. Whilst Lineker would bow out of international football in 1992, this was an era when England were blessed with an abundance of prolific marksmen. Alan Shearer, Ian Wright, Teddy Sheringham, Les Ferdinand and Andy Cole all pulled on the white of England before the '94 finals.

This was also a time when England insisted on an Englishman leading the national side. As with Robson, the FA chose a manager in Graham Taylor that had guided an unfashionable club to the league runners-up spot when he took Watford to second place behind Liverpool. Taylor repeated this feat with Aston Villa for the 89/90 season but that is where the similarities end. Before sitting in the England hot seat, Robson, as well as claiming two topflight second place finishes with Ipswich, had won the FA Cup and the UEFA Cup with the Suffolk club, while Taylor had won the Fourth Division twice.

England were drawn in a six-team qualifying group that contained 1990 foes Netherlands. In a tight three-way tussle for the two berths that would send the teams stateside, the away game against the Netherlands in

October 1993 was to prove pivotal; a draw would keep England's hopes firmly alive, on the very same night that Norway also wrapped up top spot.

In a highly entertaining game, Rijkaard had a perfectly good goal disallowed before the break but if the Dutch felt hard done by things would soon change.

David Platt, the group's top scorer, was put clear through on goal and went down as if shot by a sniper thanks to a professional foul by Ronald Koeman. The referee, Karl-Josef Assenmacher, pointed to the spot before changing his mind and awarding a free-kick, yet the Netherlands were about to be down to ten men with over half an hour left on the clock. What the watching audience had not bargained for was that the ref had given some credence to my sniper theory and felt that Koeman only deserved an 'assist' for the foul and just showed a yellow to the Dutch captain. Dorigo, in for the injured Pearce, stepped up to take the free-kick which was blocked by an orange shirt barely 6 yards away. The Dutch broke and Ronald's younger brother Erwin, who must have watched a Bruce Lee film before the game, made an appalling challenge on Paul Parker. I can only guess that the German referee was not sure which brother he had just booked so awarded nothing more than a free-kick.

Within a few minutes the Dutch were awarded a free-kick themselves in a dangerous position and although none of us watching at home needed to be told how ironic it would be if Koeman scored, ITV commentator Brian Moore felt he should. The shot was charged down in much the same manner as Dorigo's, only on this occasion the referee ordered a retake. The reprieved red card dodger chipped the wall into the back of the England net; a few minutes later Dennis Bergkamp scored to wrap up the game in the favour of the home side.

The referee had such a bad game that night, he was never chosen to officiate another international match, but that would be of no consolation to the England fans, players and especially their manager.

Just to compound Taylor's misery, who was likened to a root vegetable by some of the English press, he had agreed to be filmed for a Channel 4 programme, *An Impossible Job*, which inspired much of the feature film *Mike Bassett: England Manager*. In the documentary, that became must-see television for any football fan, Taylor looked bad, very bad, but also demonstrated how much he cared and introduced us to his catchphrase, "Do I not like that." It made him sound like quality control in a Yorkshire branch of a Greggs bakery. At least he had something original to say, unlike his assistant Phil Neal, who parroted virtually everything his boss said in a masterclass of how to be a yes man.

A month later, England still had the slimmest of chances. They had to win by seven goals away to minnows San Marino—which was possible, and hope that the Dutch lost away in Poland.

San Marino kicked off and attacked, only for Stuart Pearce to under hit a back pass and David Gualtieri to nip in and score, at the time, the fastest ever international goal. The Three Lions now needed eight. On the other side of the pitch, and luckily not caught on camera, right-back Lee Dixon burst out laughing at such an unimaginable start. To spare England's blushes, the Dutch thankfully beat Poland as England fell one goal short in a 7–1 victory.

England were not going to the 1994 finals, but for those that still harboured historic grudges, they could take small comfort in the fact that the immediate neighbours to the north and south would also miss out. Scotland for the first time since 1970 and France the second World Cup in a row, in quite unbelievable fashion.

With two games left, both at home to Israel and Bulgaria, the French only needed one point. Against Israel, who finished bottom of the section, they let in two late goals to lose 3–2. The night England trailed San Marino for over thirty minutes, France played Bulgaria. They took a first half lead thanks to Eric Cantona and although they conceded an equaliser before the break, come the final minute with the score at 1–1, they appeared to have done enough. David Ginola had the ball by the corner flag and as French fans were deciding if they could afford the trip across the Atlantic, the winger inexplicably sent in a rocket of a cross. Bulgaria picked up the ball, broke and scored, leaving Les Blues to say "Au revoir" to their American dream.

Welcome to America

For this tournament I was back at my house I owned in Salisbury and my day job was working as the area representative for a plumbing supplier. I was still working on the doors for Priestley, but pool had been replaced by the martial art of jiu-jitsu.

I had taken something from each World Cup. From Argentina, how interesting the world is, Spain, how life could be unfair, Mexico, how the saying 'Cheats never prosper' is just that, a saying, and Italy, how you must prepare for every eventuality. The lesson I was learning now is what it was like to not be invited to the biggest and best party in town, and it sucked.

The British television stations agreed, and the coverage of the group stages was sporadic. Of the games shown many were on extremely late so, combined with weekend working and two nights a week training, meant I saw very little of the group stages.

Without England or indeed any of the home nations, there was no buzz in the country.

My friends who were not really football fans but had got caught up in the atmosphere last time around, were not interested without England to cheer on and although Nick who I shared the house with was a football fan, when I got in from training, he often had not bothered to watch the games that had been shown. Despondency ruled.

The tournament had some different rules from last time, not some of the individualistic ones America had introduced, but worldwide ones. Three points for a win instead of two and a new back pass rule that had been introduced in 1992, stopping goalkeepers using their hands when the ball was passed back to them. These new rules were an overall success but still could not prevent the opening game from being a low scoring affair.

The curtain raiser was on a Friday night, so I watched a little as I got ready for work. Champions Germany overcame Bolivia thanks to a Jürgen Klinsmann goal.

What I remember from the news coverage of the time was not about the game but the opening ceremony. America, famous for its razzmatazz, was surely going to put on one to behold. Well, they put on one to never forget. First, queen of the people stuck to a sofa in the daytime, Oprah Winfrey, fell off a stage before Miss Diana 'The Boss' Ross took centre stage. The diva took a penalty from about 6 yards out, the keeper dived with no intention of saving it, the goalpost parted and she sent her spot-kick past the woodwork. Now, I knew many in America were still learning about this new 'football', but somebody surely could have explained to her that the idea was to put the little round thing between the wooden poles.

The other news of the day in America was O.J. Simpson becoming the subject of a low-speed police chase in a white Bronco. It was as if the ex-American footballer had to distract the American public from the start of the tournament in case they preferred this football to the one where hardly ever does a foot make contact with the ball.

The nearest to British representation was the Republic of Ireland returning for their second tournament in a row, still under the guidance of Big Jack, who was not the only Englishman here in a managerial capacity. Roy Hodgson had guided Switzerland to the finals.

It must have been my Saturday off as I remember watching Ireland's opening game at my friend's sister's packed house. Her husband was Irish and everybody sent up a big cheer when Ray Houghton gave them a shock lead against Italy and another one when the final whistle was blown with nobody else having bothered the scorer.

The problem with the TV companies picking the games they showed live meant that it felt like there was no momentum for the fans watching on telly. They never knew what drama or history-making moments they would miss, as came to pass in Argentina's 4–0 rout of Greece, when Maradona scored his last ever international goal.

Diego the Dope and Andres and the Narcos

A few days later, Argentina dispatched the team that they would face on such a regular basis at the finals, Nigeria, that the countries should have been twinned, and that is where the trouble started. El Diez walked off the pitch hand in hand with the nurse that was taking him for a routine after-game drugs test.

A few days later it came out that Maradona had failed his test and would be kicked out of the tournament. Suddenly, pundits and public alike all said they knew he was taking something, citing the fact that he had already served a drugs ban, along with his wide-eyed goal celebration against Greece when he ran towards the camera. While lots of people in the UK had not been able to watch the game, it was shown on Eurosport for those that had Sky; I really don't remember anybody at all airing any suspicion until the news broke. It is very easy to be wise after the event.

Maradona himself maintained his innocence, claiming it was a mistake by his personal trainer Daniel Cerrini. In Argentina he had been taking a supplement called Ripped Fast and when he ran out in the States, Cerrini bought Ripped Fuel which is the same product and virtually identical except for containing some herbs that produced the ephedrine that caused him to fail his test.

In his autobiography, Diego wrote that one day he would like to get all the evidence and present it to FIFA, even if he is sixty when it happened—how sad it was when he passed away at that exact age in 2020.

This time his international career was truly over once and for all. He had hardly played for his country since the final defeat in Italy, but after being in the stadium in Buenos Aires as a fan to witness Argentina lose 5–0 in World Cup qualifying to Colombia, he was back for the two-legged play-off against Australia and helped his country to a narrow 2–1 aggregate victory.

Thanks in part to that stunning win, Colombia were one of the front runners to claim the title in 1994, Pele even declaring they were favourites. If they could live up to the hype, it would bring much-needed relief to a country still under the influence of drug cartels, despite the death of the world's most notorious drug kingpin Escobar a year earlier. Although he and his ilk still had influence and are part of the reason why the world remembers USA '94.

René Higuita missed the finals and spent time in jail because of his friendship with Escobar, but those that point to this as one of the reasons that Colombia did not fulfil their promise often overlook the fact that Oscar Cordoba, who kept goal for the South American side at the finals, was an ever present in their qualifying campaign.

What did not come out at the time was that Higuita was not the only player who personally knew Pablo. In fact, the whole team had played a game with him at La Catherdal prison, the jail he had built and controlled, where he had agreed to spend his own prison sentence in a bizarre deal with the Colombian government. Although many of the players were not at all comfortable with this, they knew he was not a man you said no to. One of those was Andres Escobar, who was set to join Milan in Serie A after the tournament.

At the finals, Colombia started off with a shock defeat to Romania, but far worse was to come. After the game one of the Colombian players, Luis 'Chonto' Herrera, received a call from his father to tell him his brother had been killed in Medellin. In their second game they would face hosts USA in Pasadena, a chance to redeem themselves against a team they would beat easily under normal circumstances. But this was far from normal circumstances. Lots of let us just say influential people in Colombia had lost big money on their first game and were not best pleased. Things would take a darker turn.

Before the game against the United States, the coach Francisco Maturana showed up crying. The team had received death threats. The players went back to their rooms and as they turned on their hotel televisions, they must have felt chilled to the bone. Somebody had contacted them with the message that if Gabriel 'Barrabas' Gomez played, they would all be killed. Of course, even though he was a vital component of the team, the coach had no choice but to remove him from the line-up. The reason behind this threat to their own team? Lots of the biggest teams in Colombia had financial backing from the cartels and Barrabas, who retired from playing football at just twenty-four years old because of this incident, believes it was simple greed, as certain people wanted their players to be showcased on the world stage, which would then hopefully increase their value.

People who were used to getting their own way with threats and intimidation had just assumed this would work the same way with elite athletes as it did with police, government officials and anybody else they felt needed special motivation.

They seemingly forgot that this fear might also lead to normally calm and composed players making mistakes.

Colombia had the better of the game before on thirty-five minutes, a cross came into their box that skipper Andres Escobar attempted to cut out but instead inadvertently turned into his own net. This one misplaced kick would seal his fate and further damage the image of a nation whose reputation had literally and figuratively been shot to pieces.

The Americans went two up early in the second half and held on for the win that all but knocked Colombia out. Los Cafeteros won their third game, but this was not enough to see them through as one of the best third-place teams. They returned home deflated and dejected.

Once back in Medellin, Andres decided to go out, despite advice from others that had been with him in America to stay home. In the early hours of July 2, the day the knockout games started, he was shot outside a nightclub. It was allegedly by Humberto Castro Munoz, a bodyguard of Pedro and Juan Galleno, brothers who were drug traffickers and previous members of the other Escobar's cartel before they had left to join Los Pepes, the brutal gang that played a major role in Pablo's downfall.

According to eyewitness reports, whilst inside the nightclub some fellow revellers started to insult Andres. He and his party decided to leave but the aggressors followed them outside, continuing with the abuse and calling him a faggot, which greatly upset Colombia's captain. He drove over to remonstrate with the perpetrators and tried to explain that his own goal was "an honest mistake", to no avail, and was shot six times.

Unsurprisingly, in a world and country of double dealing, deceit, death and misdirection, there is more than one version of why Andres was killed that night. Some say it was a revenge killing linked to those that financially lost heavily on their national side. Others, such as 'Popeye', an ex-bodyguard of Pablo, claim it is far simpler, just an argument, a fight and Andres has simply talked back to the wrong people. The Galleno brothers were so full of themselves after their part in the death of one Escobar, they had no qualms in killing the other, even if he was a national icon.

Whether it was actually Munoz who pulled the trigger, or one of his employers, it was the bodyguard who took the fall. The brothers argued that he acted on his own without any instructions from them. The prosecutor's office in Medellin accepted this unlikely story and the brothers faced no charges, while the alleged killer was sent down for forty-three years, although he only served eleven.

Legendary Liverpool manager Bill Shankly once said, "Some people believe football is a matter of life and death, I am very disappointed with that attitude. I can assure you it is much, much more important than that." Try putting that to Andres' loved ones or teammates.

The Route to the Final

All the knockout games were shown on free-to-air television in the UK, but for many fans this was too late. Part of the fun of a World Cup is finding a team to get behind in the group stages, especially when your country is not there.

I, like many other Englishmen, even found it hard to get behind Ireland due to the start time of their games. Apart from their opener, they kicked off at 5:00 or 5.30 p.m., always on a weekday, and few bosses were prepared to let people leave early for a World Cup that many in the country simply ignored. My biggest memory of Ireland's campaign was John Aldridge and Jack Charlton arguing with the officials when trying to get the striker onto the pitch in the 2–1 defeat to Mexico. Despite this, Ireland made it through to the last sixteen, finishing second in a group where all four teams finished on four points, with Italy qualifying for the knockout stages as one of the best third-placed teams from the same section.

Most sales representative jobs I have had allowed me to plan my own diary, only going to the office when needed, but with the company I was working for at the time, it was different. At the end of the day, I always had to return to base whether I had orders that needed processing or not. Added to this I was extremely slow on the computer system, as the person assigned to teach me did all he could to sabotage me rather than help. I put it down to the misdirected anger of an internal candidate, him, not getting the job. Consequently, I often only arrived home in time to see the second half of the Irish games.

By the time they played the Netherlands on July 4, American Independence Day, a Maradona-less Argentina had been shown the door by Romania while Germany, Spain and Sweden had made it through to the last eight.

I am sure many of the country's Irish descendants were crowded round television sets, but they would fall by the same score-line as England had against the same opposition, thanks to an opening goal from Dennis Bergkamp and a dreadful error by Packie Bonner for the second.

For the second game of the day, the home crowd were hoping to send Brazil packing the same way they had the British in 1776; however, winning the World Cup for the first time in nearly a quarter of a century clearly meant more to the Samba Boys. Brazil came out on top by the only goal of the game.

While I was watching matches more regularly, the game I remember the most from the knockout stages was Bulgaria's shock come-from-behind quarter-final victory over champions Germany, thanks to goals by probably the country's greatest ever player. Hristo Stoichkov and a prematurely balding Yordan Letchkov. A result even more memorable when you consider the Eastern Europeans' tournaments history. Before coming to America, they had never won a match in sixteen attempts at the finals and even got walloped 3–0 by Nigeria in their first game in the USA.

While Brazil ploughed their way through the top half of the draw thanks to Romário and Bebeto, Italy, who had played poorly in the group stages, were the dominant team in the lower half.

The last four pitched Bulgaria against Italy and Sweden against Brazil. What was the final going to be? Was it going to be between the two most successful nations in the history of the tournament and winners of six titles between them or the final nobody, unless they had a Swedish mum and Bulgarian dad, would have predicted. Or perhaps something different altogether?

The first of the semi-finals saw Italy record their third 2–1 win in a row, all six of their goals at the business end of the tournament credited to Baggio, five for Roberto and one for Dino.

The second battle for a place in the final was the match mainly watched in Europe, apart from Sweden, by shift workers, students and the unemployed, thanks to its gone midnight start, as Brazil faced Sweden for the second time in just over a fortnight, after the group game had finished in a 1–1 draw. The Selacao progressed, thanks to a single strike from the tournament's best player Romário, to set up a rerun of the 1970 final. Sadly, the names of two combatants were the only similarities to that splendid game of football.

The Unfair Burden

Over ninety-four thousand fans funnelled their way into California's Rose Bowl Stadium, that is completely open to the elements, to watch a game that was so dire, I am sure some of them were hoping for some freak weather so it would be called off and we could all come back on a different day.

Undoubtedly millions of people in America who had not watched a single soccer game before they tuned into the final, only to witness a scoreless ninety minutes and the first final in history to finish this way, reaffirmed their belief that NFL football was the superior product. Brazil come closest to breaking the deadlock when Italy's keeper, Gianluca Pagliuca, nearly let in a weak shot that squirmed onto the post before rebounding into his grateful grip. Still, extra time lay ahead and over the three previous finals that needed the additional thirty minutes, five goals had been scored in total, yet in such a young football country, history was to be disrespected and the game finished 0–0.

The name that would be carved into the trophy as champions would be decided by a penalty shoot-out for the first time.

First up was Italian skipper Franco Baresi who sent his effort over the bar but was helped out when his keeper saved Brazil's first effort. By the time Roberto Baggio stepped up, the score was 3–2 to Brazil, Daniele Massaro also having his effort saved by Taffarel in the Brazilian goal. The Divine Ponytail had to score, or the title was Brazil's. The player whose goals and performances had led to Italy being in the final blazed his shot over the bar, then stood and stared at the ground, an image that has even been reproduced on tissues, with goodness knows what running through his mind. The World Cup had finished in the same way it had started, a penalty miss by a long-haired superstar.

Despite Baggio pointing out that two of his teammates also missed and the fact that even if he scored and Brazil had converted their next penalty Italy would still have lost, he is the one that has had to carry the awful tag of being the man who lost his country the World Cup and had described it thus: "It's a wound that will never heal."

Surely, if the final finishes in a draw after one hundred and twenty minutes a replay could be organised? Back in the day, if the FA Cup final was a draw, it went to a replay. In a time before internet, within a few days the replay was arranged, tickets were sold and people got to see the winners decided in a proper manner. With modern technology this would be an even easier task. Opponents to this idea may say what if the rematch is a draw? That is unlikely, as the fourteen FA Cup finals that have been replayed have all been settled at the second time of asking, without the need for penalties. If FIFA are worried about sponsors being too busy to attend a replay they do not deserve to be there anyway.

They could donate tickets to local schools and the volunteers that helped during the tournament, although I believe in this day and age, it would be relatively easy to sell out a replay.

With finals becoming tighter than ever, from 1994 to 2014 four of them went to extra time. Thankfully only one other, in 2006, went all the way to spot-kicks. It again featured Italy, this time against France, and while I am sure Baggio was delighted to see his country win the World Cup, I wonder if there was just a tiny bit, maybe a couple of percent, that wanted a countryman of his to fail in the way he did, to move the Italian consciousness on from that day?

I am not suggesting we should do away with penalty shoot-outs altogether, as I understand that you could not hold up the tournament for a replay at the last sixteen stage and they do add undeniable drama. Instead, just the last game, as surely no one player should be burdened with what Baggio has had to carry with him for the rest of his life.

Even though he has said how tired he was when he took the spot-kick, I am sure if you asked him today, he would have preferred the choice of a replay.

Despite 1994 having record attendances, more goals and better games than its predecessor, it is my least favourite World Cup. Not just for the poor television coverage, inconvenient kick-off times (at least to a European audience) and the lack of British representation, but also for how it ended and what it brought to a close.

Baggio was only twenty-seven years old when he played in the final and had scored twenty-four goals in his previous forty-two caps for his country. He only played another thirteen times for Italy, although he was back for France '98 playing four times.

It also ended Diego Maradona's international career under a cloud and most importantly of all was the demise of Andres Escobar at the hands of somebody that did not deserve to lace his football boots.

FRANCE 1998

Five Stars and Two Missing Magicians

If my memories of '86 revolve around Maradona and in 1990 around Gazza, France 1998 sees them revolve around five players, all of whom would play for Real Madrid at some point in their career. Ronaldo, Davor Suker, Michael Owen, Zinedine Zidane and David Beckham automatically spring to mind when the French edition is mentioned. Some memories are for good reasons, others bad, but none indifferent.

England had topped their qualifying group thanks to an excellent rear guard performance on a Saturday night in Rome, when they came away with the draw they needed, a night memorable for the image of Paul Ince with a bloodied bandage around his head and a fine performance from Gascoigne. Nobody at the time, especially Gascoigne himself, could contemplate that it would be his last competitive game for his country.

My life had changed for the better. I was now an area sales representative for Chubb Fire and was in a serious relationship. Both had started a couple of years before, at the age of twenty-nine. I was finally a grown-up. I had sold my half of the house to Nick but due to buying it just before the property crash of 1988, I walked away with just £1000. I decided to leave Salisbury and move to the much livelier beach resort of Bournemouth. All I had to my name at that time was the money, my Peugeot 205 , my clothes and a few personal possessions, such as LPs. I managed to secure a mortgage and bought a three-bedroom flat in a converted building for £50 short of £50,000.

The year before I had visited Dublin with Julie, my girlfriend, and watched England beat France 1–0 as they won Le Tournoi, a sort of World Cup warm-up event. I do not normally hold much store by these mini tournaments, but it was nice to see England win something and when you consider the other sides involved, Brazil and Italy, it looked like this England team were coming together nicely under manager Glenn Hoddle.

While many in the England team at the time have come out and said what a good tactician and reader of the game he was, and he had England playing well to boot, his man management skills were lacking, especially in comparison to Terry Venables. The previous incumbent had taken England to the semi-finals of Euro '96 and was a man that excelled at that part of the job.

Hoddle had never kicked a football in his life. Instead, he persuaded it into the back of the net, convinced it to land on his centre-forwards head or coaxed it to go exactly where he wanted it to. One of his problems was that he was still a better player than many of those in his charge and this caused unrest when he would show it during training.

England were at La Manga in Spain when he had to cut the squad to the final twenty-two and in an unusual way of doing things, he had set up five-minute appointments in his room to tell players whether they would be included. When he got to Paul Gascoigne, it all went wrong. As one footballing magician told the other he would be heading to England rather than France, it did not go down well. Gazza kicked over a chair and smashed a lamp before sending a verbal volley in his manager's direction. He knew at the age of thirty-one that he would now never have the chance to exorcise the ghost of the semi-final in Rome.

Hoddle has said that he felt Gazza was not fit enough and even though I did not agree with the decision, I do admire the manager for taking a stance. Over the years, too many in the England hot seat have selected players for squads when they clearly were not fit, normally when they were coming back from injury. He had warned him six months previously that he had to improve his fitness levels, but the manager did not feel his warning had been heeded properly and I am sure it could not have helped the player's case when he was spotted out on the town at 1.30 a.m. with DJ Chris Evans, whilst eating a kebab, less than a month before the start of the tournament.

Another mercurial talent that was left on the wrong side of the English Channel, as far as I was concerned, especially considering Gazza was not included, was twenty-seven-year-old Matt Le Tissier, the nearest Englishman that I saw to Hoddle himself. He only played two games for England under Hoddle, the first as a substitute for a few minutes against Moldova and the second as a starter at home to Italy, England's first World Cup defeat of any sort at Wembley. My friend Andy was at that game and remembers him pulling out of a challenge, so agreed with the manager that the Southampton star had not earned his place in France. A couple of months before the World Cup a rare England B fixture was arranged against Russia. One cap Chris Sutton, one of over three hundred and fifty Englishmen who have that dubious honour , went all Billy Big Boots and refused to play and as far as I am concerned rightly never played for England again. The team that night was under the leadership of Peter Taylor with Glenn Hoddle watching on, as Le Tissier, playing in an England shirt for the first time since the loss to Italy, scored a hat-trick. I thought, presumably like the three-goal hero himself, that this had earned him a place in the squad, but no, it had not. So really, what was the point of the game? I am not sure if Italy, France, Spain, Brazil, Argentina, etc. would have left not one but two players of this ilk behind. Okay, both would be a modern nutritionist's nightmare— Le Tiss was known to have a McDonald's on his way into training at Southampton—but surely it would have been worth taking one of them, if only to be used as an impact substitute?

Le Tissier himself has said that Hoddle didn't think he was fit to lace his boots and that he did not like the comparisons people made between them. Whatever the reason, I was disappointed that England were going to try and win the biggest prize in football without two talents that many other international gaffers would have included like a shot.

The Road to France

Like most World Cups changes were implemented, including the biggest one ever, with the tournament extended from twenty-four teams to thirty-two, the Golden Goal would be seen for this first time on the World Cup stage and three subs per game were also permitted for the first time.

Four countries started their World Cup finals history: Japan, Croatia, Jamaica and FR Yugoslavia, the latter two for their only finals to date. Although technically the Federal Republic of Yugoslavia, on first sight of the abbreviation I had in my head that it stood for former, had played at World Cups before as Yugoslavia and since as Serbia and Montenegro, though now in Elizabeth Taylor-like fashion had separated to became two individual teams. All this led to Dejan Stankovic becoming the only player to play at three finals for three different countries.

I was now earning decent money for the first time in my life. The job had a proper basic wage, a decent commission structure, and I was supplied with a mobile phone and a company car and no longer needed to work a second job. For the first few months at Chubb I did stay on the doors and unusually for a company of that size they had no problem with it, although once I started to see Julie, it had to come to an end. She lived in Buckinghamshire, over 120 miles away and about a two-hour drive from Bournemouth, so we mainly saw each other on weekends. I normally drove up on a Friday afternoon before leaving around 6:00 a.m. Monday morning to be back in the Southampton area, which was also part of my patch, for the start of the working week.

So, with spare cash for the first time, this was the first World Cup I bet on. I picked two teams, favourites Brazil who were around 10/3 and outsiders Croatia who I have a feeling were something like 66/1. The reason I went for Croatia was mainly down to their striker Davor Suker, who I also bet on to win the Golden Boot. It was £10 per bet. He had a decent goal scoring record in La Liga for Seville of about a goal every other match and an even better ratio for his country of almost a goal a game, so the 25/1 on offer was hard to resist. I also had another smaller bet on Marcelo Salas of Chile to top the goal scoring charts thanks in part to his performance against England earlier in the year when he scored both of his country's goals, the first something to behold in a game that was Michael Owen's debut where the youngster won Man of the Match.

Uruguay were the only previous winners not in France and missed out as South America used the nine team, one group marathon qualifying system that they still use today, for the very first time. Sweden, semi-finalists four years earlier, did not make it nor did Portugal, which seems unfathomable these days in the era of Cristiano Ronaldo.

England's last manager before Hoddle, Venables, was still in international football overseeing Australia's effort to get to France. They won six out of six on the way to their play-off with Iran who had lost two of their nine qualifiers. After a 1–1 draw in the away leg, things looked rosy for the Socceroos when they went two up early in the second half in Melbourne. The home fans must have had the smell of French coffee in their nostrils and the taste of croissants on their lips, until serial disrupter Peter Hore thought it would be a good idea to make his way onto the pitch and cut up the visitor's goal net. This caused a stoppage in play after which Iran struck twice to go through on away goals. Australia had not lost a game but had no reason to open the Bordeaux.

Scotland, like the annoying little brother you just cannot shake off when you want to hang out with your mates and who, like England, missed out last time around, had qualified again, although I think if you asked their supporters, they may class the Three Lions as their irritating younger sibling due to the fact they had appeared in five of the last six finals, three more than the Sassenachs.

Of course, Scotland ended up in a group with Brazil yet again, who they faced in the opener late on a Wednesday afternoon. It was unusually exciting for a first game. Brazil took an early lead before John Collins equalised from the spot ahead of a bizarre Tommy Boyd own goal that sealed the victory for the reigning cup holders. Boyd, whose own goal was the first at the finals since Andrés Escobar's, must have been relieved that he hailed from Glasgow and not Medellin. The Celtic man knew he might face some barbed comments when he returned home, but however vitriolic the words that would head in his direction might be, they would be easier to deflect than six bullets.

I still had a soft spot for Scotland, but over the years had come to realise that many Scots did not feel the same way about the English, which only became amplified years later when I worked with a Scottish guy called Ray at a company called Shred-it. Although we got on extremely well and he had a great sense of humour, he made it abundantly clear how we were seen in his homeland, especially in sporting terms.

After a draw with Norway, Scotland faced Morocco in a game that both sides needed to win to progress, as with the increased number of teams, only the top two in each group went through. The North Africans triumphed 3–0, meaning the Scots made their customary group stage exit after thinking they had done enough, only to discover that Norway had scored two late goals to beat Brazil for the second time in just over a year. That sent Norway through as group runners-up to the Brazilians. In fact, to this day, Norway have an incredible record when facing the South American giants. In four fixtures they are undefeated with two draws to go alongside those two victories and are the only international team that have faced Brazil more than once and remained unbeaten.

A Quiet Afternoon

While many of the games kicked off at lunchtime or the middle of the afternoon, which meant I would not see them due to being at work, I was not going to miss England's first game at this level since Chris Waddle had sent the ball over the German bar in search of Yuri Gagarin eight years ago.

It was a Monday afternoon, 1.30 p.m. kick-off. I watched it at my flat with the Chubb engineer for the area, Tim, who lived in Hamble, the best part of an hour's drive away. It was far safer for him to be in Bournemouth for the game than have somebody spotting him drive home before lunch.

Unfortunately, this was yet another England game marred by violence and some, such as Sir Brian Hayes, not only saw it coming, but also did his best to prevent it. The former deputy commissioner of the Metropolitan Police who had been recruited by the FA as a security advisor wanted the game moved from Marseille. Having the game in a troubled city with a large North African population and in stifling conditions would encourage the England fans to drink more than normal, and this was not his idea of a pleasant afternoon. He tried to convince the powers that be to relocate the game somewhere else, such as Lens, without success. After some isolated incidents on the Saturday, the following day the real trouble started. Four hundred England followers were involved in pitched battles with a combination of Tunisian fans, local youths and the police. Although, according to Hayes, on this occasion the English fans were not the instigators. He said, "Some of the African population started lobbing cans of beer at England fans, and even if England fans don't start a fight, they are up for one." He continued: "I had seen occasions when England fans had started trouble but in Marseille; I can say they didn't, from what I saw. They were heavily provoked, it was not a good experience."

In a more peaceful Bournemouth, we watched England win comfortably against a team with little or no ambition, thanks to an Alan Shearer header and a wonderful strike from Paul Scholes.

After the game, I rang the Chubb office at Sunbury-on-Thames to see if

I had any messages, as neither of our mobiles had rung that afternoon. I spoke to the woman in charge, who told me that this was the first phone call they had received in over two and a half hours. Not one rep, engineer or customer had called, and this was head office. She told me how much paperwork they had been able to process and asked when England's next game was, seemingly genuinely upset when I told her it was an evening game.

That game was on a Monday night and after an early start and a long day I chose to watch it at home on my own. For the second game in a row neither Michael Owen nor David Beckham, the only player to start all eight of England's qualifiers, were named in the starting line-up. Although I highly rated Beckham, I could see what the manager was doing. There had been a dip in his form and I agreed that a spell watching on was the kick up the backside he needed, before being brought back into the team to show just how good he was. Owen was a different story for me; he should have started both games.

In the forty-seventh minute England went one down to Romania and belatedly Hoddle sent Owen into the fray. With less than ten minutes remaining he equalised and in doing so became England's youngest scorer at a World Cup a week after he had become the third youngest player of all time at the finals, when he came on as a late substitute against the Tunisians.

His strike, however, counted for nothing, as in the last minute Dan Petrescu outmuscled Graeme Le Saux before putting the ball between David Seaman's legs to give the group's seeds the three points.

Because I only saw my girlfriend at weekends, Monday through to Thursday was footballing nirvana with a game on every night, although sometimes, like many reps, I would be doing paperwork and only be half watching the game. One such match was France against Saudi Arabia.

On a day when red was the in colour, three players were sent off in the Denmark versus South Africa encounter and one of the Saudi defenders received his marching orders in the first half. With about twenty minutes left the host nation were 2–0 up and cruising, when Zinedine Zidane decided to stamp on Fuad Amin and rightly was sent off. The player who was one of the faces of this French team nicknamed 'Black Blanc Beur' (black, white, Arab) to celebrate the team's multiculturalism had done his best to bring those three components together, when he tried to leave the Saudi number 6 black and blue that evening.

When it came to the third round of group games only one from each section was shown live, with highlights of the other later, so you had no choice of the live game. The final group to be decided would be Group G, England's. Being a Friday night, I drove up to Buckinghamshire and Julie and I settled down to watch, knowing a draw would see England through. Hoddle had taken notice of what Owen had shown him and by now had made his point to Beckham; they both started for the first time.

Less than a year since the shocking death of Princess Diana in a car crash in a Parisian tunnel, Prince Charles and Prince Harry were in the crowd to witness an England victory, thanks to two excellent strikes. The first was a powerful shot from Darren Anderton, followed by a trademark David Beckham free-kick, his first goal for his country. England looked good, so good in fact that defender Sol Campbell went on a mazy John Barnes-like run that was only stopped by the last defender and the hope that came with every tournament felt like it was based on something concrete, rather than just blind patriotism.

The round of sixteen games went pretty much as expected; well, at least according to the seedings, with five of the first six coming through their ties. Amongst these were Brazil dispatching Chile 4–1 in what I thought was going to be a far closer game. A match that created some history was France's win over Paraguay, thanks to a Laurent Blanc effort that was the final's first ever Golden Goal; whoever thought that was a good idea?

The Golden Goal simply meant that the first team to score in extra time would be declared the winner and that the game finished as soon as the ball had crossed the line whether it be the first or last minute of the traditional thirty minutes. It did not take the Wisdom of Solomon to see that this would create nervous, defensive, stale and boring extra periods. When knockout ties that were all square were approaching the final whistle, both teams would often settle for the extra period and nobody wanted to be the player who made a mistake that led to a goal with five minutes left and so little time to save the game. So, adding a system whereby if such an error was made and the game would be instantly over was an obvious step backwards.

England v Argentina Again

The last game of the knockout round was the first World Cup game I ever watched in a pub.

I had a phone call the day before from one of my customers, Mark, asking if I wanted to watch the game, a rerun of the 1986 quarter-final against Argentina, at The Malt and Hops. We had become friends when he had taken over a shop from which he was intending to sell kitchens and had found a couple of rented Chubb fire extinguishers. He rang my head office who then called me. I went out to see him and was struck by his honesty. Most people when they take over a property and find rented extinguishers in it claim they are now theirs, a sort of childlike finder's keeper's mentality. Doing the right thing paid off. I gave him an excellent deal and a friendship that is still going strong today was formed.

Mark picked me up in a taxi and after the normal questioning of the driver and what time he finished his shift—everybody I know does this—it turned out it would be around midnight. I told Mark I had put a small bet on Gabriel Batistuta, the lethal Argentinian forward known as Batigoal, to open the scoring that night. The taxi driver started calling me unpatriotic and I explained to him it was a small stake, £1, and that I was still hoping for an England victory, though I thought we would fall behind early. He was having none of it, telling me I was putting cash before country. Having worked on the doors for a decade, I knew it was best to let Loudmouth Larry sound off before coming back with one to two cutting comments once he had grown tired of the sound of his own voice. When he dropped us off about fifteen minutes before the game and as Mark was paying, I pointed out what a hypocrite he was working on the night England were playing and that somebody not even watching the game should not criticise those of us that were. I suggested he was definitely putting profit before pride.

Although the pub was standing room only, we managed to find a bit of space with excellent views of one of the televisions. The game started at a breathtaking pace and unfortunately, I was proven right when Batistuta's rocket of a penalty beat David Seaman for pace in the England goal. This led to a girl we knew from around the pub scene, who was out on a second or third date with a new fella, starting to chant "Seaman, Seaman" at the top of her voice in a pub full of blokes. She was only a tiny thing but had quite a big personality. From the look on her new beau's face, this was going to be the last time he saw her.

Michael Owen was running at the Argentinian defence and electrifying the thirty thousand in the stadium and the millions more watching on television around the world and was soon brought down for a penalty that Alan Shearer thumped home; 1–1.

Then it happened. A glorious moment in English football history. Beckham from inside his own half played the ball to Owen just inside the opponent's centre circle whose first touch was sublime, before the youngster ran at Argentina's defence once more, putting England 2–1 up with the best goal I have seen scored in an England shirt. As it went in, beer went everywhere. Just before the break Argentina came up with their own bit of magic with an ingenious free-kick routine that saw Javier Zanetti send the teams in for their half-time oranges all square. Breathtaking.

It did not take long for the joy of the first half to become a nightmare. In the same minute England had fallen behind to Romania, Diego Simeone ploughed through the back of Beckham, who, while lying on the ground, flicked his foot into the back of 'Cholo's' leg. Of course, the streetwise Simeone went down in such theatrical fashion, I cannot believe he did not get calls from the West End or Broadway offering him leading man roles. As the two men got back to their feet referee Kim Milton Nielsen showed Argentina's number 8 a yellow card before brandishing a red one in the direction of the England player. Beckham was off, England would have to play nearly forty-five minutes a man light.

At the time I remember disbelief surrounding me, rather than any foreboding of the recriminations that would come the Manchester United man's way. England defended stoutly before winning a corner towards the end of the game. It found the head of Sol Campbell who put England back into the lead. While everybody was jumping up and down, filled with delirium, I kept my eyes fixed firmly on the screen and although I could not hear anything, I realised it had been disallowed. It turned out that Alan Shearer had fouled the keeper and Argentina now had the ball and were bearing down on England's goal. I was shouting this to anybody who would listen, but nobody did. A last-ditch tackle rescued the ten men but if Argentina had scored, there would have been many bemused faces in the pub when they next glanced at the scoreboard. The final whistle meant the uphill forty-five minutes would now be seventy-five.

During extra time, David Batty was introduced in place of Darren Anderton and with neither side able to breach the other's defence, England, as they had in their last knockout game on this stage, faced the drama of a penalty shoot-out. As they had over two hours ago, the sides exchanged scoring penalties before both keepers saved the opponent's second efforts and from then on, the takers were on top. With the tally 4–3 to Argentina, David Batty stepped up and had to score England's fifth penalty. Or it was all over? Seeing him come forward I knew it was not ideal but who else was there? Of the outfield players, Scholes, Le Saux and Beckham were off the field. Only four other choices were available, all defenders, and one of those was Gareth Southgate who had missed the penalty at the European championships two years earlier when England again lost a shoot-out to the Germans. I convinced myself that Batty would score because he had the bottle to be one of the original five takers and we did not deserve to lose.

What would Hoddle have given for a player as technically gifted as Gascoigne or one with a record from the spot like Le Tissier's, who converted forty-seven out of the forty-eight he took in his career? A moment later he had a lifetime to ask himself that, when the Leeds United man's effort was saved and England once again had failed from 12 yards. One of the best games of football I had ever seen was over, albeit with the wrong finale.

The Danish referee bore a striking resemblance to one of my customers who had four cookware shops and always used this to procure a discount; no more, I thought to myself. While the consequences for this entrepreneur were minor, for Beckham the fallout was astronomical.

The papers turned on him with front page headlines such as '10 Heroic Lions One Stupid Boy' and 'Moment of Lunacy That Cost Cup Hopes'. He was vilified up and down the land with one tabloid, *The Mirror*, going as far as to print a dartboard with the pictures of those it considered villains of the day. On it were Paul Daniels, Maradona, Madonna and the goalie that dared save Batty's effort, Carlos Roa, with the bullseye being reserved for young David himself. However, far more chilling was the effigy wearing a Beckham England shirt spotted hanging from the neck outside a London pub.

I have since seen several people involved in English football saying he had to be sent off, but I still do not see that, even today. I concur more with Juan Sebastian Veron who was on the pitch for La Albiceleste and said of Simeone's actions, "It was a kind of South American thing to take advantage of a situation in the game," suggesting Beckham should not have received his marching orders. If you want to criticise Beckham, you could say he did not understand the culture of the opposition but if that is true, nor did the newspaper editors that led the vilification of a twenty-three-year-old playing in only his eighteenth game for his country. If they did, they should be ashamed of themselves. It also must have been beyond the comprehension of many that the tabloids either persuaded or at the very least confirmed that he deserved this level of hatred. If they responded in such a manner when they had had time to reflect on things, how many of them would have controlled their emotions in the heat of the battle?

Yes, as fans we have the right to criticise footballing mistakes, but they must be tempered. Many players that played for England in this era have mentioned the fear factor that came with playing for their country, so you can only believe that the way Beckham was treated has contributed to that.

More Entertaining Fare but Not Always So

Each of the quarter-finals offered up something for the neutral, even Italy's scoreless draw with the hosts. Roberto Baggio, who had hardly been seen in an Azzurri shirt since the USA four years earlier, stepped up and scored his penalty in the shoot-out, as he had done in the group game to rescue a draw against Chile. Now, shorn of his ponytail, he wisely took his side's first kick rather than the fifth. Whether success erased the feelings from four years earlier, these personal redemptions were not enough to see his team through to the last four.

Up next was the five-goal thriller in which Brazil edged out Denmark, before the game in Marseille where the Dutch faced Argentina rather than England. In another highly entertaining game with extra time looming and both sides having had a player sent off, Dennis Bergkamp took three touches, all with his right foot and with the last scored a quite exquisite goal, one of the finest seen on any stage, to book a semi-final berth and in doing so making me doubly happy. I was happy Argentina were out and I had bet on three or more goals in the game.

The last game of the round was a real shock to many as Croatia got the better of Germany. The Eastern Europeans were producing the form I had hoped for. Late on in the first period Germany's Christian Worns saw red, and the debutants took full advantage of the extra pair of legs, netting three times without reply in the second half including the last from Suker in his quest to be the top scorer in France.

In the first semi-final the Dutch lost on penalties, and have over the years proven they are nearly as useless at this rather important part of the game as England. Brazil were now just one game away from becoming the first team to retain their title on two separate occasions.

With England out and the combination of being underdogs and my £10 riding on them saw my adopted team Croatia now needing to beat the hosts. Just after the break, this far-fetched dream suddenly looked a reality when Suker scored, as he had done in every one of the knockout rounds, to give his side the lead, thanks in part to Lilian Thurman sitting a little too deep and playing him onside. If they could keep a clean sheet, they would be playing in a final in their very first World Cup. Within a minute though, they had conceded when Thurman made amends, scoring with a right-footed shot. It was the only game of the one hundred and forty-two he played for France in which he had scored, before incredibly scoring again, this time with a wicked left-foot shot from outside the area before sinking to his knees and putting his hand to his face in a memorable celebration that had the look of 'What have I done?' I enjoy celebrations like this, pure, spontaneous ones. I am even okay with the trademark ones such as Cristiano Ronaldo's jump in the air or Alan Shearer's arm aloft as he wheels away. They still seem passionate. I am not so keen on the choreographed ones such as the over-rehearsed handshakes; they take away from the moment for me and lack real emotion.

Four minutes after going ahead, France had a free-kick in line with Croatia's box and as the ball was whipped in, Laurent Blanc and Slaven Bilic were involved in a scuffle that saw Croatia's number 6 end up on the floor holding his face after some naughties from the French centre-back.

Blanc received the first red card of his career, one that meant he would be suspended for the final. France now had to play sixteen minutes with ten men and hope they could hold on which they did before lofting Thurman shoulder high at the final whistle. The replay told a different story. The contact in the incident was minimal and certainly not on the part of his face that Bilic implied. Whether or not you thought Blanc should have walked, I did not and remember, I was supporting Croatia; you had to feel sorry for the Frenchman, missing the final for contact that would not have seen a one-legged pirate go down after three bottles of rum. Everybody I spoke to felt FIFA should have used video evidence to overturn the ban, but unfortunately for Blanc they did not.

The Tale of Two Team Sheets

Come the final and as normal, it was broadcast on both ITV and BBC, but with the BBC starting their coverage much earlier. It was their silver fox, Des Lynam, that broke the unbelievable team news: Ronaldo was out, Edmundo was in. O Fenómeno was the focal point for Brazil and was such an incredible talent it was unthinkable for him not to be leading the line for his nation. He had won the Ballon d'Or in 1997 and had netted four times en route to tonight's game. Still only 21, he would have been searching for his thirtieth goal for his country. Then Des kindly informed us that a new Brazilian team sheet had been handed in and in a move that would annoy fantasy football managers of today, Ronaldo was suddenly playing.

The opening goal of the final was scored by Zidane with a header from an Emmanuel Petit corner. The Frenchman had not only risen for the ball but for the occasion, something he would do so many times in his career, as he did with his spectacular volley that clinched the 2002 Champions League final for Real Madrid from a cross by Roberto Carlos, one of his opponents in the final. Just before the break the Brazilian defence proved to be slow learners. Another French corner, this time supplied by Youri Djorkaeff from the other side of the field, brought another Zidane header and the lead had been doubled in what looked like a copycat version of their first strike.

France continued to look the better team but gave a possible lifeline to the Samba Boys when Marcel Desailly received a second yellow card halfway through the second period for a foul on Cafu. Not only were France going to have to play out the remainder of the game a man light but also without both of their first-choice centre-halves, something on a normal day against a Brazilian team that contained Ronaldo, Rivaldo, Bebeto and Roberto Carlos would have spelt disaster. This though was no normal day. Brazil could not find a way through. When the ten men broke in injury time you sensed they would score long before Petit guided the ball into the back of the Brazilian net.

Cue huge celebrations. A million people on the Champs-Elysees that had images of the victors projected onto it for the first time since the end of the Second World War.

The enduring story, however, especially in the football mad nation of Brazil, was just what had led to a team sheet being handed in with Edmundo named on it instead of their star man?

Ronaldo's parents were in France. Somebody had the bright idea to put the estranged couple in a house together and the inevitable happened, a fight occurred. A player already carrying the hopes of two hundred million people on his shoulders and contending with a knee injury now had a family feud to deal with.

The Brazilians were staying at the reputedly haunted Chateau Grande Romaine and on the day of the game as the team were resting, Ronaldo was in his room with Roberto Carlos. Carlos watched his team's star player start to shake and have convulsions before falling to the ground. Hurriedly, he left the room and fetched Edmundo, who was the first on the scene and had woken the other players who were understandably concerned by what they had heard. When they left for the stadium, they were not concerned whether he would be playing but more for his life. It was not the best preparation.

Ronaldo, who had been taken to hospital, arrived at the ground and declared himself fit to play, meaning Brazilian manager Mario Zagallo, who was the coach last time Brazil were defending champions back in 1974, decided Edmundo was out, Ronaldo was in.

The Brazilians appeared more focused on their talisman than the opposition and when he had a collision with Barthez, their concern was palpable. Was he going to be okay? He was, but could do nothing to defend Brazil's title.

Since that day speculation has abound around the tale of the two team sheets and many theories have been put forward. One is that the Brazilian Footballing Federation overruled the coach and that it was their decision, not Zallago's, for Ronaldo to start. Another is that he was drugged, possibly by the French. Yet another is to do with Nike who had signed a sponsorship deal with the Brazilian Federation in 1996 worth a huge £100 million. Reportedly, it meant the sponsors could arrange five friendlies around the world wherever they chose on top of Brazil's already packed schedule. Was it beyond the realms of possibility that a company that held this much sway could become involved in team selection and insist that he played? Many thought not. The most outlandish in my opinion is that Brazil sold the game for hosting rights, although according to Edmundo in the documentary *The Three Musketeers*, most taxi drivers have embraced this theory.

England, Croatia, Brazil and twenty-eight other countries failed while the French won their first ever World Cup. The victory brought the divided country together and although it appears not to have lasted, it showcased the power of football.

JAPAN AND SOUTH KOREA 2002

The Mouth of Hod

2002 was the first World Cup held in Asia and the first to have joint hosts, Japan and South Korea.

England started the qualifiers under the leadership of their very own Ally MacLeod, the extremely popular Kevin Keegan, who was hoping to be involved for more than the twenty-six minutes he managed as a player at the finals. Hoddle had left the job in unusual circumstances.

His charges had dropped points in two of their three qualifiers as they attempted to make it to Euro 2000, so the knives were at least out of their sheaths if not being sharpened by the British press. It was hardly surprising that if the players he was awarding international caps to felt his interpersonal skills were lacking, then his relationship with those paid to write about England could also have been better.

It was against this backdrop and in the run-up to a Wembley friendly against world champions France that Hoddle gave a telephone interview to Matt Dickinson of *The Times*. If Ollie Holt had not been away, he would have been the one asking the questions and maybe the ex-Swindon Town and Chelsea boss would still have been in charge of his country at the 2002 tournament.

Dickinson had recalled Hoddle talking previously about his religious beliefs and also felt there was mileage in discussing the faith healer Eileen Drewery, who Hoddle had brought into the England set-up.

During the chat Hoddle revealed his thoughts on reincarnation and according to the journalist said, "You and I have been given two hands and two legs and half-decent brains. Some people have not been born like that for a reason. The karma is working from another lifetime." Hoddle denies he said this and instead had discussed why some people are in poverty. The battle lines were drawn and even British Prime

Minister Tony Blair was asked on the *Richard & Judy* show whether the England manager should be sacked. Did the daytime duo really expect to get a thought-out, honest, considered reply from a politician to such a question? They must have known he was going to say whatever he thought the public at large wanted to hear.

Soon Hoddle was gone; it was becoming clearer and clearer how much influence the press in England had when it came to the country's footballing gaffer.

Howard Wilkinson stepped into the breach as caretaker before England fans were given the antidote to the Yorkshireman, who would have made an announcement that you had just won £20 million on the lottery seem like a twenty-year prison sentence, with the appointment of the bubbly Keegan.

Beckham, Beckham and more Beckham

England started their qualifying campaign at home with a 1–0 loss to Germany, thanks to a fourteenth minute strike from Dieter Hamann. This was the last ever game played at the old Wembley and it felt like the Liverpool midfield had succeeded where the Luftwaffe had failed over fifty years before and had destroyed the symbol of English football recognised around the globe, especially when Keegan resigned after the game.

This meant England were again looking for somebody to fill the void and they eventually settled on the Swede, Sven-Goran Eriksson, the first foreigner to take up the challenge. While accepted by some, others were against him from the start, purely because he was born in Torsby instead of Torquay.

When the final round of qualifying games arrived, England were facing Greece at home while Germany hosted Finland. Both teams sat at the head of the group on sixteen points, England with a superior goal difference, thanks to an amazing night in Munich that ended with a final score of Germany 1, England 5, that had helped Sven be accepted by even his harshest critics. If England could match Germany's result, they would be heading to Asia for the finals. If not, it would be their great rivals advancing while the Three Lions would have to take their chances in the play-offs.

England trudged down the Old Trafford tunnel (Wembley was being rebuilt) at half-time, trailing by a goal to a team with nothing to play for.

In the sixty-sixth minute the manager sent Teddy Sheringham into the fray. He made an immediate impact when he headed the equaliser with his first touch from a David Beckham free-kick, yet within a minute the home side were again behind against a team to whom they had never lost.

Beckham, now his country's captain, was having an amazing game. It was as if he had a vision that if he had not been sent off in St. Etienne, then England would have not only have beaten Argentina but would have won the last World Cup. He was doing everything within his power to make up for it by keeping them in this one.

He was everywhere and England were awarded free-kick after free-kick. However, their specialist, nor indeed any of his teammates when he was kind enough to lend them the ball, could find a way past the Greek keeper. During injury time he had one last chance. England were awarded a set-piece in a central position about 30 yards out. Beckham struck the ball with his right foot, sending an unstoppable shot into the back of Greece's net, while I simultaneously let out an almighty scream that was half delight and half relief and one that would have scared any children in the flats above or below mine. Fittingly, when the final whistle blew the ball was with Beckham and with Germany being held to a goalless draw, England had qualified by the skin of their teeth.

Beckham's effort that day, especially in the final quarter of the match, is the finest individual performance I have ever seen on a football pitch. He was so good that if all ten of England's outfield players could play like that at the finals, Eriksson could have picked Benny Hill in goal and they would still have been crowned champions. He popped up in so many positions I half expected him to be serving burgers in a concession stand and marshalling the car park. If anybody who had abused him three years earlier did not forgive him that day, they simply did not have a soul.

During qualifying on the other side of the world history was being made. Australia beat Tonga 22–0, a record score for a full international and a game in which Archie Thompson scored his first international goal as a late substitute.

The record only stood for two days before American Samoa were demolished by the Socceroos. Manager Frank Farina had evidently been saving Thompson for this game and the striker scored thirteen times, another international record, in a 31–0 victory. Australia unsurprisingly topped their section with a record of played four, won four, scoring sixty-six goals and conceding none. They overcame New Zealand in a two-legged play-off before facing Uruguay for the last spot at the finals. Australia flew to South America with a slender one goal lead to defend. When they attempted to exit Montevideo airport they were abused, jostled and spat on by a group of Uruguayan supporters. The two-time world champions took the game by three goals to make it a full house of previous champions appearing in Japan and South Korea.

Keane on Change

The World Cup started on the last day of May and that month, I am sure to the relief of my neighbours, I moved to a new flat. Unlike my last one which was a conversion, this was brand new and now I had a bit of money to furnish it to a decent standard. That included a new television, a big boxy thing that was about 28 inches, not the top of the range, but the best I had owned and far from the 70-inch flat screens of today. Two of the first things beamed into my home on it were football-related but for off-the-field activities.

In a stunning press conference, Michael Zen Ruffinen, the Secretary General of FIFA, accused Sepp Blatter of mismanaging funds and called for him to resign. Naturally, slippery Sepp was not going to go that easily. He said that he could not leave as he had been elected so had to stay until the next congress which was due to be held just before the tournament and that was where his future would be decided. The vote unbelievably went Blatter's way; well, unbelievably to honest people. I am not going to go into the corruption that has dogged FIFA any more than that, as there are plenty of books that cover what went on in great detail.

There was also another scandal involving an Englishman, an Irishman, Will Smith, some missing kit, Muhammad Ali and a loyal Labrador named Triggs.

Roy Keane was the Republic of Ireland's skipper as they qualified via the play-offs, overcoming Iran after emerging from a group that included Portugal and Holland. This was probably the best team they had sent to the finals, but trouble had been brewing for some time before they landed on the Japanese island of Saipan. Over the years, the Irish international set-up had been seen by many as a joke. According to Keane, when they arrived the hotel was up to scratch but nothing else would pass muster. I mentioned the film *Mike Bassett* earlier, that in part took inspiration from Graham Taylor's fateful spell in charge of England; well, it appeared the Irish set-up had watched the film and thought it was a 'how to' manual. The skips containing the training gear and footballs did not arrive on time, the training pitch was rock hard, as nobody in the Irish contingent had thought to inform the FIFA liaison officer when they were due to train (so he could arrange to have it watered), and the Irish keepers declined to take part in a training session because they were too tired.

Before the qualifying campaign, Keane had sat down with English-born manager McCarthy and they had agreed to up the ante on the off-field arrangements for the national side, or so the Manchester United skipper thought, and therein lies part of the problem. Keane was used to doing things the United way under a boss, Alex Ferguson, who would push for perfection both on the pitch and off it.

All this Three-Stooges-style preparation became too much for Keano who told McCarthy he wanted to leave, but then changed his mind. The manager then pointed out that he had already contacted Colin Healey as a replacement, so Keane stuck with his decision to go.

However, just before they had to fax their final squad to FIFA, Ireland's captain was given one last chance to stay, which he accepted. In true Irish fashion this was not to be the end of things. In the meantime, Roy had given an interview to Tom Humphries of the *Irish Times* and unlike some other stories in this book, there are no recriminations aimed at the journalist involved; well, not by Keane anyway, who had seen a final copy and signed off on it, unwittingly adding to the farce he saw as the Irish international set-up.

On the long flight to Japan, he had watched Will Smith in the film *Ali*, for which the actor received an Oscar nomination for his portrayal of thrice heavyweight world boxing champion Muhammad Ali. One particular scene caught the attention of Ireland's number 6. When Ali was being pressured by those closest to him to accept the draft for the Vietnam War and telling him he would not have to fight, he still refused.

He was not prepared to bend on what he believed in and despite his own indecisiveness, Keane drew inspiration from the film—don't compromise on the things you believe in.

After dinner on the day the interview was published, a team meeting was called. McCarthy asked a couple of times if anybody had any issues and Keane, sensing an ambush, kept quiet until his manager addressed him personally about the interview and then lambasted him for faking an injury to get out of the second leg against Iran. Now having watched him time and time again for United, I can believe anybody who suggested Keane had lost his temper with them just a bit too quickly, but fake injury? I just cannot see that. And apparently this was what sent him over the edge.

When Roy spoke, he cut into McCarthy with as much venom as any punch Ali ever threw. "You're a fucking wanker. I didn't rate you as a player, I don't rate you as a manager and I don't rate you as a person. You're a fucking wanker and you can stick your World Cup up your arse. I've got no respect for you." Keane, who picked up countless team and individual awards, was never going to count being named as the Irish poet laureate among them.

This outburst sealed his fate, and he was soon making his way back to Cheshire where he found his house besieged by the press. His wife told him that with the circus going on outside she had not been able to get out of the house and the dog had not been out for a couple of days. So, after a little time with his kids, he took his four-legged friend for a walk and that is how Triggs ended up as one of the lead items on the news. In the end, I played as many games at the 2002 World Cup as the skipper of the Republic of Ireland.

No Nights in Japan

This was the first World Cup in which I gave serious consideration to attending. I had now split with Julie, so was back in Bournemouth full-time. When I had first moved to the town, I made a large group of friends at a local gym but none of them were really football fans. I thought about asking Mark if he wanted to go but with two small children, I knew he was probably a non-starter. Another friend who was not a regular at the gym was Andy, but he was a football fan and a Manchester United supporter. A trip to Japan, where England were based, was not going to be cheap, but I had a secondary reason. Jiu-jitsu had originated in that country so it had stoked my interest in visiting. Andy said no, his primary reason being the hooliganism that had accompanied all-too-many an England fixture. I told him I understood but was also convinced that very few hooligans would travel that far. I had also watched a documentary on the Japanese police and how they were going to deal with anybody looking for fights instead of footie. Alas, it was to no avail. Meaning that when the tournament started with champions France against Senegal who were a 9/1 shot, not for the competition but just to win this game, I was in my new flat. After the tournament had gone off peacefully, Andy told me he wished we had gone.

For the first time I would witness a World Cup with no evening start times. The games were generally played in three time slots: 7.30 a.m., 10:00 a.m. and 12.30 p.m. Consequently, I, and many others in Europe, would miss a great deal of the games.

My work was going well, so well that Salisbury became part of my patch and was now creating so much paperwork that I needed a day a week working from my home office to deal with all the admin. I scheduled these days to coincide with games I didn't want to miss. Even though I was practically my own boss, my work ethic was not going to let me sit at home for the best part of a month.

I had backed Spain to win the tournament and had put £50 on France to win their opener. I was friends with one of the other reps in our team named Mark who also liked a bet.

I agreed with him to put £50 each on France to beat Senegal to start our 'World Cup fund' and I very nearly changed my mind at the last minute. But no, we were in this together and I staked my money on the French. For me this was a very large stake so it was best to stick with the plan. Well, that went well.

It was 1990 all over again—minus the red cards as the little fancied Africans took the spoils against the world champions 1–0.

On the Sunday, England were facing Sweden in a mid-morning kick-off. I went with kitchen fitter Mark to a venue he suggested in Southbourne that was laying on breakfast before the game. It was a hotel, so far less crowded than the pub we went to four years previously for the

Argentina game. The build-up within the English press was dominated by two things. One was Eriksson facing his home country and whether his loyalties would be divided. The other point of interest was the England captain's foot.

In April, during a Champions League quarter-final, another unwelcome Argentinian intruder came into David Beckham's life. Aldo Duscher made an appalling two-footed studs-up tackle that saw the United number 7 unable to continue. He had fractured a small bone in his foot and suddenly a new term was thrust upon the English public. He had damaged his metatarsal and a word that had been reserved for emergency rooms and insurance claim forms was now making its way into polite dinner conversation, onto factory floors and drinking den debates. Would David be ready for the World Cup? Well, ready or not, the match against Sweden was his first game back and he lasted for just over an hour.

For the first time, FIFA had extended the number of players in each squad to twenty-three. The rumour around this increase from the normal twenty-two was that Brazil could now include the injury-prone Ronaldo, which they did, and Italy could include Baggio who had similarly struggled with injuries, but they did not. Whatever the reason, this extra place meant England took a chance on Becks.

With all the games being daytime affairs, I had to pick and choose the weekday matches I would watch and one of them was Brazil against Turkey. The Samba Boys had experienced a hard time in qualifying, losing six games, finishing third and level on points with Paraguay, behind Ecuador and section winners Argentina, who they trailed by a massive thirteen points.

Still, with an attacking triumvirate of Ronaldo, Ronaldinho and Rivaldo, I was excited to see what they could produce. In stoppage time in the first half, the deadlock was broken, not by one of Brazil's three Rs or even by one of their teammates; instead, it was Hasan Şaş who gave the Turks a surprise lead.

After the break, Ronaldo spectacularly flung himself at a cross to equalise and near the end Brazil were awarded an undeserved penalty. In a tournament remembered by many for the poor officiating, Luizao was bearing down on goal and was pulled at by Aplay Ozalan, who rightly saw red for a second bookable offence. But a penalty? The foul started 5 yards outside the box! Within minutes the Turks again would be upset with the referee and as Rivaldo was waiting to take a corner, Hakan Unsal blasted the ball at him, hitting the Brazilian number 10 on the thigh, who then went down clutching his face. Unsal was sent off for a second bookable offence and Rivaldo received no on-field sanctions. At the time, the extremely talented Brazilian was playing for Barcelona and was one of my favourite players to watch, so I was saddened and disgusted by his actions. Play-acting is something I really despise about the modern game and while he did receive a financial penalty, that was it. What does a hit in the pocket matter to players earning megabucks? A two-match ban and the humiliation of making him read out a statement admitting his guilt and that he was trying to cheat would I believe have been a more fitting punishment.

Most football fans don't like this form of cheating and those that look to knock the beautiful game often start by citing this behaviour. The sooner the players realise, the better. Yes, you should give your all but it should not be a case of win at all costs.

England vs Argentina Third Time Lucky?

England's next outing was against Argentina, a Friday lunchtime affair. The media talked about 1986 and 1998, revenge for the country and redemption for the captain. The two previous encounters were in the knockout stages, and whilst this was not, the 'Group of Death' nature of the contest meant it was just as hyped as those that had come before.

Although it did not provide the same level of entertainment, it did have a familiar feel when Michael Owen, who had earlier hit the post, was hauled down for a penalty. As Beckham stood ready to take it, a player offered to shake hands. It was of course Simeone, who this time was ignored by a four-year-older and possibly twenty-year-wiser man. If only that had happened the last time they had met on this stage, who knows what would have transpired? Beckham struck it low and hard. I thought for one awful moment Argentina's keeper was going to deny him as he appeared to have hit it straight at Cavallero. Instead, he had wrong-footed him. The only goal of the game meant England had beaten Argentina at a World Cup for the first time since 1966, to triumph in the only true intercontinental rivalry I can think of.

By the time the group stage of the tournament had finished, I had seen all the fixtures of only two teams, England and Brazil. I knew if both teams won their next tie, the game I had enacted so many times on my 'flick to kick' game would be a reality.

The opening part of the tournament had thrown up several surprises. Co-hosts Japan and South Korea had both won their groups. Korea's unbeaten start was helped by a victory over Portugal who had two players sent off. The Portuguese duo would not be the only players to see red against the Taegeuk Warriors. Argentina had failed to make it through and France, the team defending their trophy, had finished bottom of their section with a solitary point and had failed to score a single goal. Quite a remarkable feat when you look at who they had available at the business end of the pitch, Thierry Henry, David Trezeguet and Djibril Cisse, who had all finished as the respective top scores in their day jobs in the Premier League, Serie A and Ligue 1 in the lead-up to the tournament. True, Les Blues were missing Zidane for the first two games, but at the time, they could still call themselves world, European and Confederation Cup champions. Maybe the other twenty-two players in the squad could have helped out a little more.

To get to the game with Brazil, England had to face Denmark in a Saturday lunchtime affair, which meant a late breakfast out with Mark before another victory, this time 3–0.

Results were now going more or less as expected.

The Italian Rob

That was until the South Koreans faced Italy. Even though I missed it at the time I feel like I was there, thanks to the reaction from anybody with Italian heritage I have ever mentioned this game to.

Italy had gotten this far by finishing second in their group, only winning once against Ecuador, but were still fully expected to make their way to the last eight.

Whether Ecuadorian referee Byron Moreno had revenge on his mind, was bribed or just not up to the job, only he, and maybe a select few others if it was option two, knows.

My Italian friends have explained to me in great detail, far greater than is needed, to be honest, how the referee pulled off the biggest heist since Michael Caine, three Mini Coopers and a bunch of cockney likely lads stole some gold bullion in *The Italian Job*. Firstly, he awarded the Asian side a dubious penalty, but Gianluigi Buffon foiled his dastardly plan by saving it. So, instead he allowed, let us be generous and call them challenges from the Koreans, including Del Piero getting an elbow in the chops and Maldini a kick in the head, to go unpunished. The game finished level so extra time was needed. Moreno still had more work to do. He gave Totti a second yellow card of the night for simulation. The problem was, he was 40 yards away at the time. How could he spot this if he missed flying elbows and kicks from a few yards away? Italy also had a Golden Goal wrongly disallowed before the home side struck the one that did count.

Italy is a wonderful country, full of amazing history and delicious food, but when things go wrong sometimes the Latin temperament goes all Roy Keane.

Ahn Jung-hwan's winning goal had consequences that neither he nor even Eileen Drewery could have foreseen. At the time he was playing in Italy for Perugia. The next day, the club's owner, Luciano Gaucci, sacked him, saying, "I have no intention of paying a salary to someone who has ruined Italian football." A week or so later he changed his mind, but by then the Korean hitman, possibly fearing an Italian one, decided Japan was a better home for the time being. Papers in the country produced headlines such as 'Ladri', which translates as thieves, and the sticker album that introduced children of all ages to the stars of many a tournament got involved.

Panini, who hail from the same part of the country as Enzo Ferrari, a man not known to take defeat lightly, decided to withdraw stickers of the Italian team from circulation in protest.

Possibly the country that knows a thing or two about corruption had a point on this occasion. In 2002 Moreno was the man in the middle for one of local side's Deportivo Quito games. He added minute after minute of injury time until they scored an extremely late winner. At the same time, he was standing for political office in the city. The suspicious might find a link. The Ecuadorian FA certainly did, banning him for twenty matches. The following year he got another suspension before hanging up or possibly selling his whistle.

Some might go quietly into retirement, not bothering the headline writers ever again. Not good old Byron. Instead, in 2010 he managed to get himself arrested at JFK airport in New York with 6 kilograms (around 13 pounds) of heroin stuffed down his underpants, for which he received a thirty-month jail sentence. I will leave the last word to Buffon. "Six kilos of dope? He already had them in 2002, but not in his underwear, in his body."

England vs Brazil vs Mexico

It had finally arrived: England versus Brazil in a World Cup, not in a final as I had hoped, but only two short steps away. Although I was excited in the build-up to the game, I was also despondent. I just believed England would lose. This was unusual; I am normally an optimist, always believing the team I support can get something out of the game even if they are three down going into the closing stages. But I had been watching Brazil and England closely and for me the outcome was a foregone conclusion. I was so certain that I had booked a holiday starting the day after the game.

I had been walking through Bournemouth the day England drew 0–0 with Nigeria and saw in a travel agent window a deal for a fortnight in Mexico for just over £600, a real bargain. By now I had visited the country on several occasions and had started to fall for it, but each of these previous trips normally set me back over a £1,000. I called my friend Steve to see if he could take holiday at such short notice and he could, so I just had to convince my boss. It was always hard to get them to let you take holiday when you were one of the top performers; whatever I sold affected my manager's bonus. He presented the normal "I need your figures" argument, until I pointed out that I had already nearly hit my target for the month and with over a week to go I was going to blast through it, so reluctantly he agreed.

When people found out they said, "You're going away during the World Cup, you'll miss it." I had to point out that Mexico did have television sets, and colour ones at that. "But what about the celebrations if England win it?"

"We won't," I would counter. Brazil had won four out of four, scoring thirteen times with a front three that were on fire. England had won only half of their games netting five goals, with as many of them being scored by centre-halves as strikers.

Friday morning came and I found myself dressed for work stood in The Litten Tree pub in Bournemouth's Old Christchurch Road with my friend Max similarly attired in a shirt and tie and ready to go straight to work after the game.

With a 7.30 a.m. kick-off neither of us were drinking alcohol. That was for two reasons. Firstly, we had to work afterwards, and secondly, we did not fancy it.

Despite all my pessimism, England did have Owen and when Lucio made a mistake halfway through the opening stanza, he pounced to give England the lead. While we were not drinking, plenty of others were and Max, who was not a big football fan, was rather surprised to be covered in beer. Being 6 foot 4 inches tall he took more than his far share. As the celebrations died down, he asked if we could watch the second half back at my flat. Just before we jumped in our cars to make the short journey on eerily quiet roads, in what would normally have been the middle of rush hour, Brazil conjured up an equaliser. Beckham jumped out of a tackle on Roberto Carlos in the Brazilian half, later claiming that he believed the Brazilian would not be able to keep the ball in play and would have conceded a throw to England. To many observers it looked more like he was protecting his foot. Whatever the truth it was the wrong decision, as Gilberto Silva did keep the ball within the white lines, and it quickly found its way to Ronaldinho who ran at an England defence who did not know what to do. He then fed the man who would not be welcome in kebab shops around the globe, clinically picking his spot past David Seaman.

Looking at the benches, I was even more convinced England would be in the air at the same time as me. The Samba Boys could introduce the likes of Kaka and Denilson, while England had Darius Vassell and a thirty-six-year-old Teddy Sheringham as their game changers.

Five minutes into the second period and Brazil had a free-kick out on England's right and some distance from goal. It was too far to shoot so only a one-man wall was formed. Ronaldinho took it and the moment that has been subject to conjecture and debate ever since was a mere second away. The ball floated over Seaman who had come off his line and the Brazilian scored one of the best or luckiest free-kicks ever seen. This goal meant two of the three Rs had scored in all five of Brazil's matches thus far.

Ronaldinho himself has claimed he meant it and certainly celebrated like he did. Others, however, have poured scorn on that scenario and even within the Brazilian camp there was not 100% agreement. Kleberson said although he believed it was done on purpose others in the squad disagreed.

I still am unsure, but I do know that a player capable of receiving a standing ovation in Real Madrid's Bernabéu whilst playing for Barcelona would certainly be capable of it.

The Three Lions were given a lifeline when Ronaldinho was sent off with over half an hour to play and then Ronaldo was substituted with twenty minutes left. Two of Brazil's three danger men were now off the pitch and England still had a man advantage. Seemingly to even things up, Eriksson decided to take Michael Owen off for Vassell. He also threw on his Teddy to no avail. Brazil were through, England were out and Steve and I were not going to be out of the country while the rest of England celebrated winning its first World Cup in our lifetimes.

Ronny's Redemption

The next day I was up at stupid o'clock to pick Steve up to make our way to Gatwick to fly away for our two weeks in the sun.

We got to the airport bang on schedule, checked ourselves and our luggage in and then instead of doing what I have done every other time I have flown, make my way through security, we spotted a bar showing Spain against South Korea and decided to watch some of the game. Maybe the Spanish would have the tie sown up by the break and we would saunter through: they didn't so nor did we. Sometime during the second half, we suddenly realised that we needed to make a move and headed for security as quickly as possible. Some kind people let us jump the queue as our names were being called. We found our gate number and were running as fast as we could down a travellator when I spotted a group of four people ahead, standing motionless on it and blocking both sides. I called to them to watch out, but they had the reaction time that you would expect of somebody too lazy to walk to a plane. It was too late and I was on top of them. I am not sure if I went through them or over them, but I emerged the other side still on my feet and without any real loss of momentum. We made it to our flight—just. We got plenty of dirty looks as we were the very last passengers on board, which I understand, but as far as the human roadblock is concerned, all people have to do is follow the well-known and extremely simple etiquette of standing to one side!

With all that pre-holiday excitement my memory of the game is blurred. I cannot remember if we saw Spain's two disallowed goals and it was a couple of days before we knew my pre-tournament bet was no longer running and Spain had gone the same route as the Italians, thanks to a penalty shoot-out. The Egyptian referee was about as popular in Spain as Mr Moreno on the other side of the Mediterranean Sea.

At the time, the football pools were doing a sweepstakes where you picked the four semi-finalists and when Turkey added their name to that of Brazil, Germany and the Koreans, I am pretty sure the number of winners would have been declared as zero.

Being the closing stages, the last four games of the tournament were played in a more sociable lunchtime slot for European audiences; the only trouble was that we were no longer in Europe, so we were again back to early morning kick-offs.

The semi-finals saw normality return as Germany and then Brazil made their way to the final. I had missed these games but had to keep up my run of watching the decider. It began at 6:00 a.m. local time. The plan was that I would wake Steve and we would watch it in the room. That morning he was dead to the world, so I decided to head out and try and find somewhere within the hotel to watch the game. I wandered towards the main restaurant, but the doors were locked, so I went round the back and found the staff entrance where several of them were gathered around a television. Thinking I wanted breakfast they gestured for me to come back in an hour when they would open. With a bit of Spanglish, we established that all I wanted to do was watch the game and I found myself welcomed in with a cup of tea and a bowl of fruit, as we saw Ronaldo score twice, one of them coming from an Oliver Kahn fumble in the German goal. Earlier, the keeper had been outstanding on the night and indeed during the entire competition. In fact, he was so good that he won the Golden Ball as the tournament's best player. Brazil had won seven out of seven to become world champions for the fifth time. Ronaldo had completely laid the ghost of France, scoring eight goals to win the Golden Boot.

Beckham had his absolution, Ronaldo had his redemption along with the title, but if Becks had not jumped could England have produced the victory the nation so desperately craved?

GERMANY 2006

Aussie Winners and Losers

The 2006 tournament held in Germany was the first one that the defending champions were not granted automatic qualification for. I have no idea if this was already in the pipeline or decided on after France's debacle in Asia, but by then, I had happily seen England win a major international tournament.

England had come through the group stages with a 100% record, defeated France in the last four before doing it the hard way in the final against the hosts. Full-time and the scores were level, meaning that extra time was required. With the end of the added period ominously close, Johnny Wilkinson's right boot gave England victory against Australia. England were world champions, in rugby. Nevertheless, this had given me a taste of the incredible pride that you feel when a sporting team you support, your nation, lifts the trophy which means they can call themselves the best in the world. I remember the day, even the date, November 22, 2003, with amazing clarity. I recall making bacon sandwiches before the morning start for my mates Eddie, Scott and Danny at my flat. I also remember watching Manchester United beat Blackburn in a lunchtime kick-off, as my mind kept wandering back to the rugby and I was unable to concentrate on the game at all, such was the impact of the victory.

Several nations made their FIFA World Cup debut in Germany, including Ukraine, Trinidad and Tobago and the Ivory Coast. The Caribbean nation was the last qualifier along with the winner of the Uruguay versus Australia tie, a rematch from four years ago.

The Socceroos were playing in their fourth consecutive play-off to try and secure a place at the finals. This time they played the first leg away, which they lost 1–0. Mark Bresciano scored the only goal of the return fixture meaning for the first time ever, a finals place would be decided via a penalty shoot-out. To the delight of the eighty-two thousand spectators packed into Sydney's ANZ Stadium, the home side prevailed. Guus

Hiddink, who had taken South Korea to the 2002 semi-finals, had guided Australia back to the World Cup for the first time since 1974.

Since the last tournament, I had left Chubb after seven years to work for an on-site shredding company which I now look back upon as a mistake. I aggravated my back problem at work and the boss refused to let me record it in the injury book. That day, I knew I needed to leave and a few months later I was gone. I set up my own fire safety company in partnership with my old engineer from Chubb, Tim.

I was again in a serious relationship, this time with a girl named Gail who lived in Bournemouth, less than ten minutes' walk from my flat.

T&T Tickets

Before the draw was made for the finals, I discussed with my friend Anton the possibility of going to Germany. We looked at the FIFA website; I now had my first computer since my ZX81 at school, and the only option left was centred around Trinidad & Tobago. The way tickets were allocated at the time was that you purchase one to follow a team but had no idea who the opponents would be. We thought about it, knowing we would need to find accommodation in three different cities as the idea of groups being contained over one or two cities was now a distant memory. In the end, we decided against it, our logic being that we may end up seeing three one-sided games.

When the draw came out, we did have a moment of regret as one of the teams paired with the Soca Warriors was of course England. At the 2004 Euros a young man named Wayne Rooney had played extremely well and looked like he could carry the team virtually single-handedly to the final; that was, until he was injured in the quarter-final defeat to hosts Portugal. Hope was high of England doing well in Germany.

However, when Eriksson named his England squad all my normal optimism left immediately. Paul Scholes was not in it, having retired from international football after the last Euros. He was tired of being the makeweight in England's midfield and often played out of position to accommodate the big names that the manager seemed to be in awe of, such as Steven Gerrard, Frank Lampard and Beckham.

Plenty have said these next two statements before, but they bear repeating. Gerrard and Lampard did not get the best out of each other and if Scholes was Spanish, Italian, or French he would have over a hundred caps.

I would have built the midfield around Scholes. Gerrard would have got the nod over Lampard, who would be an excellent sub to bring on if the Liverpool legend needed replacing in a game or a great alternative if he had a dip in form. When I worked with Ray the Scotsman, he said something to me that resonated. "The problem with the England players is when they go into the dressing room and see their names on the back of the shirts." I knew what he was getting at. Under Eriksson, too many players had become virtually impossible to drop, especially if they had a big media profile. While it's great to have a settled side, players can get too blasé about their place in the team and the understudies a little despondent.

No Scholes was no surprise but up front is where the selections lost me completely. He named only four forwards in Owen, Rooney, Peter Crouch and Theo Walcott. The main two strikers were carrying injuries. Owen had played less than half an hour of football in 2006 prior to the side's two pre-tournament friendlies and Rooney, like Beckham four years earlier, had injured his metatarsal with around eleven days less recovery time before England's first game. While I argued earlier for taking a possibly unfit Gazza, it is one thing taking an impact player who is not at his sharpest, but it is a completely different beast to take a pair of strikers who were not match fit and could break down at any minute. Maybe you do this if you have plenty of other strikers in your squad that you trust but taking only four meant if these two were out at the same time, England were relying on Crouch and a largely untested Walcott.

I did not have too much argument with the first of these two; having a 6-foot-7-inch centre-forward could be a useful differential.

Walcott was another story. The highest level at which he had played was the Championship for Southampton, before being signed halfway through the season by Arsene Wenger at Arsenal. Eriksson had never seen the youngster play before selecting him in the squad on Wenger's recommendation. The England manager was listening to a Frenchman that had neglected to give him even one minute in a Gunners shirt, whilst deciding on the best strike force to help England win the trophy for the first time in forty years.

It sounded like a plot from a *Carry On* film and in part it was. If you were going to take Owen and Rooney, you had to have a plan for both being out at the same time. I would have added Jermaine Defoe along with Darren Bent who had just averaged a goal every other game for a Charlton side that despite finishing in the bottom half of the Premier League, had seen Bent finish the season as the top scoring Englishman in the division. Some youngsters such as Owen and Rooney for England and Whiteside for Northern Ireland can handle the pressure, but it would soon become clear that Eriksson did not believe the seventeen-year-old Walcott could. He gave him his international debut with a twenty-five-minute run against Hungary in England's penultimate game before the finals but left him on the bench in the 6–0 thrashing of Jamaica in their next game. In fact, he did not play for England again until virtually two years to the day of his debut.

When I saw this squad, I was desolate. For the first time in my life, I felt England had no hope whatsoever of being crowned champions. I knew the Three Lions would not emulate their cousins that prefer an oval ball to a round one.

The hosts kicked off the tournament with a 4–2 victory over Costa Rica, the first goal being an absolute stunner from German full-back Philip Lahm. My money was again riding on Spain and I cannot remember who I picked for the Golden Boot. All I know is that it was not the eventual winner, Germany's Miroslav Klose, or anybody in the England squad.

England Arrive in Style—Magazines

I did not have to wait long to see England's opening tie; it was the first game the very next day, a Saturday. With normal German efficiency, the first two rounds of group games were played at 2:00 p.m., 5:00 p.m. and 8:00 p.m. UK time, with no odd variations as had happened at previous tournaments. For the last round of group games, the matches kicked off at 3:00 p.m. and 8:00 p.m.

England scored early through an own goal to take the points, with Owen and Crouch up front. Five days later England faced Trinidad & Tobago with the same strike force and Rooney was named on the bench for the second game in a row. With just over half an hour remaining,

England's new wonder kid was sent on in place of the old version, with the 'wonder why I am here kid' nowhere to be seen.

Although the game was goalless at the break, it should not have been. Crouch was unmarked on the penalty spot from a Beckham cross and went for a spectacular finish that was so bad, well, there are just no words. Close to the break John Terry made a fantastic goal line clearance to stop the underdogs taking the lead.

It took until the eighty-third minute to break the deadlock, when Crouch scored, unsurprisingly with a header, and a fine Gerrard effort wrapped up the points. England were through with a game to spare and Eriksson bizarrely decided to start the game against Sweden with the two strikers that had come into the tournament carrying injuries. I can only presume it was to keep Crouch fresh for the first knockout game, as he had played the full ninety minutes in England's first two games, plus he had received a booking. None of the other forwards had completed a full game to that point.

Of course, the accident that had been waiting to happen did and just like an episode of the hospital drama *Casualty*, it occurred in the first minute. Owen injured his knee and was replaced by Crouch. Owen and Rooney, players that Eriksson had decided were fit enough to win the World Cup, played a grand total of one minute together in Germany. That the sides shared four goals, one of them being a stunner from England's Joe Cole, seemed secondary once it became clear that Owen's tournament was over, and Walcott was not going to play whatever the situation. England had topped the group, but at what cost?

While knees, toes and injuries were making the headlines for England on the pitch, there was plenty to read about off it as well. Not to do with the players themselves, but their wives and girlfriends, or as they became known—the WAGS.

Staying in the elegant spa town of Baden-Baden in a separate hotel about 20 miles from the players HQ, things went wrong from the get-go. Somehow the FA had booked the players' other halves and families into the hotel where most of the press tasked with covering them would also be putting their weary heads on pillows.

This was the age of *Hello!* and *OK!* magazines as many of the orange squad saw the whole exercise as a giant photo opportunity and unfortunately showcased why so many countries despise the Brits abroad. Their lack of self-awareness as they appeared to mistake Baden-Baden for Benidorm was truly remarkable.

How did this come about? Apparently, the manager and his skipper lobbied for it. Eriksson, being the bronzed Adonis of football management, conducted two affairs that had made the papers, one with television presenter and fellow Swede, Ulrika Jonsson and the other with FA employee, Faria Alam. His partner at the time was the famous-for-being-famous Nancy Dell'Olio. I have a hunch that she did not trust the man—someone who appeared to cover more ground in the search for illicit female company than Lampard and Gerrard combined at the heart of England's midfield—to be out of her sight for up to a month, so she pushed for it.

Also, by now David had a Mrs Beckham, one Victoria Adams, or to provide her proper title, Posh Spice. Posh was somebody who never knowingly missed a chance for publicity.

But these two alone could not attract that much attention. They had the supporting cast of Cheryl Tweedy (Ashley Cole's girlfriend), Colleen McLoughlin (Rooney's squeeze and future wife) and Elen Rives, Lampard's partner. There were others, adorned with designer handbags and oversize sunglasses that screamed "leave me alone, oh you are, I only meant for a little while, please come back". I know several of the players have come out and lambasted the press for their behaviour, and I understand nobody wants to see their loved ones criticised, yet these stories don't write themselves. Other players in the squad such as Gary Neville and Rio Ferdinand saw it as a problem. Therefore, it was.

What is the most disturbing part for me is that some of the magazines that fill this space years later are still lauding this month of mayhem, but expecting them to see the reality of the situation and how these young women confirmed the worst stereotypes about the English—that they drink too much and like ripe fruit don't travel well—is a bit like asking a vegan to eat a glorious ribeye steak, a rare one at that.

Much to the relief of employers across the land, none of England's games landed in the early slots on a weekday and I must confess I did not see a single group game that started before five o'clock. We needed to grow our fledgling company. This meant that I missed the first goals on the World Cup stage of the two players considered to be the finest of their era. When Argentina systematically took apart Serbia, Lionel Messi scored the last of their six. A day later, as if he knew that their names would be linked throughout their careers, Cristiano Ronaldo slotted home a penalty for Portugal.

The Referee That Scored a World Cup Hat-trick

As usual, I had been following Brazil and as they expectedly took apart Japan in Group F's last pair of games, the real drama involved Australia, Croatia and the English referee Graham Poll.

With players on the Australian side having links to Croatia, such as Mark Viduka and Zeljko Kalac, and monikers to match, Poll needed to make sure he noted down carefully the nationality as well as the name of any player who transgressed the rules.

As the closing stages of the game approached the 2–2 score-line it meant the Socceroos would be the side to progress. That outcome looked even more likely when he sent off Croatia's Dario Simic with five minutes left for a second yellow card offence. Within two minutes, however, the main advantage had disappeared when Brett Emerton received his marching orders, also for a second bookable offence. Poll clearly understood the rules. If player is booked twice, you then show him a red and he must leave the field of play immediately. Croatia's Josip Simunic became the third player of the tie to be booked twice in the ninetieth minute but this is where everything went wrong for Poll. He kept the red firmly in his pocket, as if it had a sticker on the back that read 'Only to be used twice per game', despite at least one player highlighting his mistake. Then right on the final whistle as the Socceroos bundled the ball in for a disallowed goal, the sticker must have fallen off; he again showed the Croat a yellow card, his third of the game, and then a red, thereby becoming the first referee to complete a hat-trick at the finals.

How did this happen? Surely if the man in the middle makes such a monumental error, one of his assistants would have helped him out of the Poll-size hole he had just dug for himself. In a radio interview a few years later, one of those assistants, Glenn Turner, said that Poll had told him and the other assistant to just concentrate on the game and not to note down any incidents. I get the impression he thought Poll was a bit arrogant. I cannot remember if Turner had spotted the error and just hung him out to dry or missed it as well.

The referee who would forever be remembered for this three-card trick has said he did not realise his mistake at the time and in fact had written down Australian number 3 in his book by mistake. To be fair, Simunic had been born in Canberra and spoke with an Australian accent, but the contrast between the red-and-white-tablecloth style of Croatia's shirt and the gold of Australia should have saved the day. Poll, like Clive Thomas many years before him, found his World Cup adventure at a premature end and his dream of officiating the final gone forever. People around the world remember his error, rather than Australia qualifying for the knockout stages for the first time in its history.

The other team that I had started to follow more than most was Mexico. Gail and I had visited two or three times by now and were both in love with the country, so when she turned up for our date the night El Tri were due to face Argentina in the round of sixteen, I tried to persuade her that this was good Saturday night entertainment. She was not impressed. We had arranged to go to a local music venue, Mr. Kyps, to see an Elvis tribute artist called Suspiciously Elvis. In this scenario, when she feels I am out of order, she has this look that descends on her face, one that puts me in mind of one of Paddington Bear's cold, hard stares. As I didn't fancy being lonesome that night, the fake 'King of Rock 'n' Roll' defeated Argentina, who in turned beat Mexico in one of the tournament's best games, apparently.

Missing this game became more of an annoyance the longer the tournament went on, as I did not find the football on offer particularly entertaining. Starting from the last day of the group games and ending at the semi-finals, on only three occasions did both sides register a goal.

The next three games all ended with a 1–0 score-line. England edged out Ecuador in a poor game thanks to a Beckham free-kick, with an unhappy-looking Rooney ploughing a lone furrow up front and completing a full game for the first time in over two months.

The next two games were more memorable but not necessarily for the right reasons.

Portugal and Holland kicked off at 8:00 p.m. and then again two minutes later when Mark van Bommel received a yellow card for a lunge on Ronaldo. The Battle of Nuremberg had begun. The game ended with four red cards and sixteen bookings in all and although Sepp Blatter criticised the referee, no player received three yellow cards. Ronaldo had to be substituted in the first half after some over-the-top treatment and even as he sat on the bench with tears in his eyes, any sympathy England fans felt towards the 21-year-old would be gone within the week.

Gross Decision

The very next game in the round of sixteen threw up more debate and annoyance in Australia, as well as in my household.

With the closeness of the knockout games, I thought the Socceroos tie with Italy would finish goalless.

I had possessed a phone account with Totesport for years, so one quick call and my bet was on. They had an offer that made me choose them over popping into a high street bookie. They would pay out on both the correct score as the clock hit ninety minutes as well as the score at the end of injury time.

At the end of the ninety minutes the score indeed was 0–0, so if either team bagged a winner, it made no difference to my bet. I had won. In injury time, Italy, who had Marco Materazzi sent off in the fiftieth minute, were pushing for a winner, wanting to avoid playing an extra thirty minutes a man light.

Fabio Grosso attacked down the Azzurri's left, beat his man and found himself inside the penalty area, before Lucas Neill slid in. Grosso, like an Italian Charlie Chaplin, fell over the prostrate defender to claim a rather undeserved penalty which Francesco Totti converted. Italy were through, Australia, rather unfairly, were out. I was in profit.

It was only when I opened my statement that arrived in the post that I found only two of those beliefs to be true. My bet was marked as a loser. I called the bookmaker to point out their error, thinking it was just a simple mistake and they would rectify it while I was on the line.

I explained the issue to the girl who answered the phone, and she checked her computer and said the correct score was 1–0. I agreed but then recounted the terms of the offer and explained that Totti's goal was in stoppage time. She checked the computer again and told me it was scored in the ninetieth minute. "No, it was not, it was in injury time," I replied. She was not budging so I suggested asking round the office to see if anybody had seen the game, words that fell on deaf ears. I explained the offer of the company she worked for again and was just deciding whether I had called on a 'bring your child to work' day when I came up with an idea. Check the Spain versus France encounter which also had an injury time goal. She huffed as she checked and was all pleased with herself when the last goal of that game was also recorded as being scored in the ninetieth minute, not realising this added strength to my argument. I pointed out that it sounded like they were recording all injury time goals as being scored in the ninetieth minute, rather than the actual minute, and therefore, were at fault. She gave me the website they used but said there was nothing that could be done. So, a quick check and indeed, every goal I could remember that was scored in injury time had been erroneously recorded as have been scored in the ninetieth minute, meaning that never once during the entire tournament did they have to honour the offer.

At the time, the internet was not the beast it is today, there was not the plethora of football sites now available that I could use to argue my point, so a bit like Australia, no matter how I aggrieved I felt, I just had to let it go.

Swiss Dismissed

With the Aussies feeling hard done by, they were joined by the Switzerland team in the room marked 'How did that happen?'

The Swiss topped their group ahead of France and were the only team thus far that had not conceded a goal. They were facing World Cup debutants Ukraine who had lost their opening game 4–0 to Spain. At the end of one hundred and twenty painfully dull minutes the score was 0–0. Penalties would be the deciding factor. Whether you agree or not that this is a good way to decide a game, it certainly is dramatic. Normally. The Swiss contrived to miss their first three spot-kicks to lose the shoot-out 3–0, but bizarrely were going home with four clean sheets in their four games. I presume Jose Mourinho was aghast.

Germany, Brazil and France, who ended Spain's twenty-four game unbeaten run and my tournament winner bet, were the other teams that made it through to the last eight.

Saturday Afternoon's All Right for Fighting

England faced Portugal and the two young Manchester United teammates Rooney and Ronaldo would face each other, both desperate to reach the semi-finals. Of course the two players that over the years would become headline hoggers were involved in the game's defining incident.

I watched the game with my friends Danny and Gary, the latter of these not being a football fan, but like many others, someone who would be drawn in for the big games. Gary wanted the atmosphere of a pub, so we choose Bar Vin in the town centre and being a 4:00 p.m. Saturday afternoon kick-off, it was rammed with hardened drinkers, hardly drinkers and fervent fans alongside the fair-weather ones.

Thanks to Eriksson's squad selection he started with only one striker, Rooney, with Crouch held in reserve on the bench in case plan A did not work. Something many an England fan expected. Portugal, however, were without Deco and Costinha, suspended for their part in the Dutch debacle.

After a poor goalless first half, early in the second Beckham had to be replaced due to injury but worse was just round the corner. Rooney was clearly becoming more and more annoyed, not a good look for a young player who could reach boiling point quicker than Gordon Ramsey.

Just past the hour, with no help up front, the simmering kettle that was Rooney boiled over. He battled gamely with two opponents before stamping on the most delicate part of Portuguese defender Ricardo Carvalho, right in front of the referee.

Ronaldo was on the scene almost immediately, getting in the official's face, so Rooney pushed him away before the referee showed the England number 9 a straight red. The third England player sent off in the nation's last five World Cup tournaments, all of them Manchester United players. Was this coincidence or linked on some level to the abuse United players would get when on international duty for their country? Just coincidence. Wilkins was before the anti-United sentiment had set in, Beckham was petulant and unlucky, while Rooney's error appeared to be based on the pure frustration of having to play the lone role.

Ronaldo was caught on camera winking at the bench. I cannot remember if it was shown during the game or after but he was mercilessly booed by virtually the whole pub for the rest of the game.

England now had no strikers on the pitch, so Eriksson took off Joe Cole and replaced him with Crouch. In one ten-minute period, three of England's probable first choice penalty takers had left the field of play.

Just as the atmosphere around us appeared to be calming down we heard a crash and within a couple of minutes a guy was being thrown out and we spotted another one in an England shirt with a towel on his head. He had been bottled. Some of the people in the pub were not going to forget today in a hurry, whatever the outcome.

With no score at the end of normal time, the game was extended by thirty minutes. England still had one substitution left, Portugal had none. England needed pace if they were going to catch their opponents on the break, their most likely route to victory, something Walcott reputedly had plenty of. It was time for Eriksson to back his judgement on the youngster or admit to the world he had made an error with his squad selection, which could quite possibly lead directly to England being knocked out. It was the latter, keeping his substitution back until the hundred and nineteenth minute when he sent on Jamie Carragher. The Liverpool defender was obviously going to be one of the first five penalty takers, against the team that had knocked England out in similar fashion at the last Euros. Two of the others would be Gerrard and Lampard, players that took them for their clubs. Hope, that most deceitful of emotions, still lingered.

First up was Lampard who was denied by Ricardo, Owen Hargreaves scored and then Gerrard also saw his effort saved. Portugal had missed twice so when Carragher appeared for his turn they led 2–1. He scored but had not waited for the referee's whistle. A retake was ordered and as the Liverpool man tried his luck once more, he changed his technique; a little stutter was added into his run. Instantly I knew he would fail and fail he did. Ricardo was the first goalkeeper in World Cup history to save three penalties in a single shoot-out.

Still, if Paul Robinson could save the next spot-kick the day was not over. A wine-shirted player stepped forward; it was Ronaldo. Of course it was. He sent the England shot stopper the wrong way condemning this team to join those of Italia '90, France '98 plus the Euro teams of 1996 and 2004, who all faltered and then failed from the spot. All the previous misses were not as bad as Carragher's for me, even Waddle's effort he sent over the bar sixteen years before. Carragher had performed the biggest sin; he did not follow the simple rule of playing to the whistle, heaping extra pressure on himself. A bloke next to us said he had at least had a profitable day; he had had a tenner on Portugal to win on penalties or more accurately, England to lose that way. While some others made snide comments on their way out, those of us who had suffered before understood his logic. England win and that's great; however, if they made him suffer for over two hours and then some, he would at least be compensated for the gut-wrenching feeling that witnessing your country defeated in such a manner can deliver.

Ronaldo's wink drew the obvious headline 'The Winker' and this time the British press made the Portuguese youngster the villain of the piece, instead of the player he shared a dressing room with at Manchester United.

Even if England had got through, Rooney would have been suspended, meaning they were effectively down to one striker. England's challenge would in reality have been over that afternoon in Gelsenkirchen. Or more accurately, when Eriksson named his unbalanced squad.

Danny but No Daniel

After the game Danny and I made our way back to my flat, while Gary headed off to see his girlfriend.

My flat was a few hundred yards' walk from Bournemouth's football stadium. On an out-of-season Saturday night this normally would have no significance but today, thanks to Reginald Kenneth Dwight, it did.

I had received a phone call during the week asking if we could supply fire extinguishers on a short-term rental to the football stadium as Elton John was playing his first gig in the town for over twenty years and they needed additional cover.

I had delivered them on the Friday and been presented very kindly with two complimentary tickets.

Under normal circumstances, I would have surprised Gail with these, but she had flown off that morning to Sardinia for a girls' holiday.

I was confident that Danny or Gary would want to join me but as Gary was busy it left Danny as the only real option. He was to be my concert companion, or so I thought. Once back at my flat he decided he would prefer to watch Brazil take on France that evening and promptly crawled into my spare bed for a nap. I rang round a few other mates, but many already had arrangements and others sounded decidedly the worse for wear. Another problem would be the traffic, although I could walk to the stadium; anybody taking up the offer would still have to get to me, and the traffic would be horrendous as the venue does not have great access.

As I did not fancy going alone, I settled for watching the Brazil game with Danny. I could not wake him, so I watched the game sitting at home, with two Elton John tickets burning a hole in my pocket and my slightly inebriated buddy snoring softly in the background.

To make matters worse it was a poor game that the French won 1–0. Not even Brazil's Ronaldo who had become the final's all-time top scorer when he netted his fifteenth against Ghana could find a way through the French defence. Agent Wenger's plan was now becoming clear. While Zidane, Henry and others would take care of the likes of Brazil and Spain, his mission was to get England out of the picture.

Heading for Italy

The last four was an all-European affair and the first of these pitted the hosts against Italy. That summer had been baking hot and a friend called Bear invited me to watch it with him in his garden.

Although he is small and hairy that is not the reason for his cuddly moniker; he is from Iran and it is an abbreviation of Behrouz. It was a decent game with the Italians' two fine goals at the end of extra time providing the most dramatic of finales.

During the game I received a couple of texts—WhatsApp was not a thing yet—from Gail, telling me what a fantastic atmosphere there was in Sardinia. She and Julia had found a bar full of Italians to watch the game with. They were on the side of the island that does not get many English tourists so with Gail being blonde and blue-eyed, it was assumed at first that they were German until Gail managed to explain that they were English, so would firmly be behind their holiday hosts. To get Julia to agree to watch a game was no mean feat. Once when she was single, she declared her next boyfriend was not allowed to like football and I had to explain very carefully that she might be waiting a very long time if she stuck to that rule.

The final pitched Italy against France who had overcome Portugal thanks to a Zidane penalty.

I called Anton to watch the game but being half Italian, he had decided to fly to the country to watch it on television with his dad in the small town of Carsoli and enjoy the celebrations if Italy won. By now the girls had moved from Sardinia to nearby La Maddalena Island, so once again I was getting annoying messages about a great atmosphere. This time they were watching on a big outdoor screen and for one evening, the sleepy picturesque town was transformed into a mini San Siro. The World Cup was even starting to rub off on Julia, who was watching her second game of the week, although during the first one she did disappear shopping at some point and upon her return and realisation that the game would be extended by thirty minutes, she started to grumble.

The game started off with a brace of early goals, Zidane opening the scoring from the spot courtesy of a Materazzi infraction on Florent Malouda, before the Italian defender made amends by equalising with a precise header. The game unfortunately did not kick on from this spectacular start. When the end of regulation time arrived, the score remained 1–1 between two teams that had only lost one game between them of their last fifty-one combined internationals. The goal scorers knew their names would always be linked to this game, but not for the reason they believed at this point.

With the game in the second period of extra time, it was stopped for an off-the-ball incident and the cameras panned to Materazzi, face down on the turf. Moments later replays revealed what had happened. Two players were walking up the pitch in conversation, Zidane started to jog away before turning and out of the blue forcefully head-butting the Italian defender in the chest. Zidane saw red, the concluding act of not only his international career but his footballing one. Much had been made in the build-up of this potentially being his last match of any sort and of the superstar leaving his mark on the game. Nobody realised it would be a head-shaped one on Materazzi's chest. I know many players and managers try and put pressure on the referees when decisions go against them even when the man in black is 100% correct; however, French boss Raymond Domenech sarcastically clapping the decision made him look a complete fool. If I was not already hoping to see France beaten for other reasons, Wenger and knocking out Spain and Brazil, as well as the fact they were French, I think I may well have changed my allegiance at that point.

With neither keeper beaten in the closing minutes it became the second final that would be decided from 12 yards.

France shorn of their main penalty taker went down 5–3; Italy were champions for the first time since 1982, cue maniac celebrations in Carsoli, La Maddalena and the rest of Italy.

It came out later that the Inter Milan player had insulted Zidane's sister and that is why he lost his temper and planted his head firmly into his opponent's chest. I know some people in France see this as a normal reaction but for me this was Zidane putting himself above his teammates, as well as his country. He only had to stay calm for a few more minutes. Denying Materazzi a winner's medal would have hurt him far more.

Having worked on the doors of pubs and nightclubs for many years I know people will say stupid and hurtful things to try to provoke a reaction. However, most of us manage to keep our tempers in check for a lot less money than Zidane picked up on a weekly basis. Rooney was wrong, Zidane was shameful. Both had cost their country.

SOUTH AFRICA 2010

A New Continent

England were now under the stern leadership of Fabio Capello who had taken over the reins in 2008 when the FA appointed a second foreign coach. He led them to South Africa in a canter but not as easily as Holland and Spain who won every one of their qualifying games.

Australia and New Zealand would be appearing at the finals for the first time together. The Socceroos had moved from the Oceania Football Confederation to the Asian Football Confederation in 2006, which had two immediate benefits. They would play more competitive matches, which was instantly apparent as their biggest win in qualifying was 4–0, meaning the team would be better prepared if they made it through. In addition, they would also avoid the dreaded play-off.

The main controversy I recollect from qualifying came in the European play-offs. FIFA declared there would be no seedings. The eight teams would just go into a random draw to determine the four two-legged ties that would decide who made it to South Africa. However, once France and Portugal were involved, seeding was introduced, much to the annoyance of the smaller nations. Yet for the Irish, the most dubious deed still awaited.

The Republic of Ireland, who had finished second in their group to defending world champions Italy, drew the 2006 runners-up who post Zidane were in decline. At the Euros the year prior, France had secured only one point whilst finishing bottom of their group.

Despite losing the first leg at home 1–0 the Irish were still confident when they played the return four days later, a game they won 1–0 to send the tie to extra time.

In the additional period Malouda took a long free-kick into the Irish box, where one or two French players appeared to be offside. No whistle came, enabling Henry to take three touches and set up William Gallas for the goal that sent France through. The problem was that the Arsenal man appeared to mistake the lush green grass of the Parisian pitch for a basketball court, as the first and second of these touches were with his hand. Shay Given in the Irish goal pursued the referee like a hungry dog might a kindly butcher, but nothing was to be done.

When the draw was made and England were paired with Algeria, Slovenia and the United States, they were installed as third favourites behind Spain and Brazil. *The Sun* ran the headline 'EASY', using the first letters of the four countries, changing United States to Yanks. England was proving to have a collective memory problem, needing to remind itself of their failure to qualify for the last Euros whilst finishing third in their section.

As with what seemed every World Cup England had an injury problem. Rio Ferdinand was named captain despite having had an injury hit season for Manchester United in which he played in less than half of their games. In the team's very first training season on South African soil he suffered ligament damage to his left knee that ruled him out of the entire tournament. At least Capello had time to call up a replacement in the uncapped Michael Dawson, who, unlike Walcott, had operated for several years in top flight football. Although I had been vehemently opposed to his inclusion four years earlier, I now believed he deserved a place in the squad. Walcott had played over one hundred times for Arsenal, many of these in European competition, and had become the youngest player to score a hat-trick for England. While he stayed home, Emile Heskey and Jermaine Defoe joined Rooney and Crouch as England's forwards. By now Crouch had netted twenty-one times for his country but the joke doing the rounds was that he only scored against countries that pointed at the sky if an aeroplane flew overhead. Again much was expected of Rooney who although still just twenty-four was one of the most capped players in the squad.

The fact that the manager was approaching players who had said they were done with international football was another concern. He persuaded thirty-two-year-old Carragher, who had not played for his country since 2007, to return to the fold and went after the thirty-five-year-old Scholes who was still winning trophies with Manchester United. It just reeked of desperation. Not so much propositioning a player of Scholes' class to return after six years or asking two players who had never played for him, but the last-minute nature of the calls. Scholes was not approached until a month before the tournament and did not feel he was given long enough to decide. If he had been given longer he stated his answer may have been the same as Carragher's.

This was the first time a World Cup would be hosted in Africa. While Sepp Blatter has done a lot wrong, the tournament being granted to a soccer-crazy continent made up of over fifty countries containing more than a billion people was one of his better moments, even if the way it came about was not.

The world's critical eyes were on Africa as a whole, the continent being a virgin to staging anything of this magnitude in the sporting world, no previous World Cup or Olympics. In 1995, they had staged the rugby World Cup in South Africa, which Nelson Mandela cleverly used to bring black and white together. However, the World Cup was on a completely different level.

By now I was living with Gail and we had purchased our first house together. We considered going as it looked a stunning country but there were just too many obstacles on this occasion. I had gone my separate ways with Tim but still owned Abacus Fire and was busy rebuilding the customer base, after splitting it with him. We now also had a rather large mortgage and had heard disturbing reports about how safe it would be to travel to South Africa.

I knew to ignore the over-sensationalised headlines such as those in the *Daily Star* about a 'World Cup Machete Threat' but did feel the need to do some research when other more respected news outlets highlighted the danger. I had a South African secretary working for me and asked her opinion. She told me some places were fine, but others would be too dangerous to leave the hotel. My friend also had a South African employee and I got pretty much the same story from him. For us, this was not a great situation. I know some people are happy just to stay in a hotel and only go to a main tourist street; we, however, like to explore and attempt to understand the culture of where we are. So, going against our natural instinct, we decided to look at packages, which were horrendously expensive. The last deciding factor was that if we followed England, we would possibly be travelling thousands of miles once we had arrived and might be going from a safe to dangerous place overnight. We decided to target Brazil as the place to fulfil my childhood ambition.

South Africa had decided on the German start times and would use only three for the entire tournament. Due to very little time difference to the UK, most match days had three slots—12.30 p.m., 3:00 p.m. and 7.30 p.m.—and as the tournament progressed only the latter two would be utilised.

However, what was not as well organised and something fundamental to the game was the ball. It was made by Adidas but for many of the players it might as well have been fashioned by a drunken old man. Before the tournament had even started the Jabulani was garnering unwanted headlines. Many players came out and criticised the way it flew through the air. Brazilian keeper, Julio Caesar, even likened it to the type you buy in the supermarket.

The first game pitched hosts South Africa against Mexico in the Johannesburg Stadium, aptly named Soccer City. Now, while normally I would have been rooting for the underdogs, on this occasion and because of my growing allegiance to Mexico—we had started to give serious thought to moving to the country—I was hoping to see them lose. Stephen Tshabalala scored with a rocket of a shot for the hosts and the sheer joy that erupted from the stadium almost changed my mind. Rafael Marquez, who was the best known of the Mexican squad in Europe, thanks to his tenure at Barcelona, equalised and when the tie finished with no more goals, I felt pleased for both teams.

However, the noise coming from the stands annoyed me. The whole World Cup was played against the incessant drone of the vuvuzela, a large trumpet-like contraption that made every game sound like there was a giant swarm of bees present. I not only found the din itself irritating, but also the fact that it drowned out any other crowd noises such as chanting or the oohs and aahs that normally accompany a near miss.

While the infernal instrument irked many, it was defended at the time as part of the culture of South Africa. It has been claimed that it was first invented back in the 1960s but also that it was used many years before by the Zulu to announce victories or summon people. Thankfully, it was banned for Brazil four years later.

The next day, England were ready to take their first three points as they marched through their 'easy' group. Partnering Terry in place of Ferdinand was another player whom Capello had never selected before, a footballer I rated highly, Ledley King. Unfortunately, the Spurs man was injury prone and of course by half-time he had to be replaced by Carragher. England's cup was only forty-five minutes old and they were already playing with a fourth-choice centre-half. Gerrard had opened the scoring after four minutes and from that point onwards England's challenge faded.

With half-time approaching, Clint Dempsey hit a speculative shot from around 30 yards out that somehow beat Rob Green in England's goal. Was this a case of the ball dipping and swerving unexpectedly as several of the goalkeepers had warned us it would? No, it was just an awful mistake by the keeper who I and many others did not believe should have been playing. Nick from Salisbury texted me before the game and said that he believed Joe Hart should be between the sticks. While I agreed he was probably the best keeper in the squad, Capello had failed to prepare him properly; he had only played three times for England, all of those being for just half a game. Hardly the preparation needed for the white-hot cauldron of a World Cup. At half-time I received another text and when I managed to get past all the swear words, the gist of the message from my fed-up friend was that he was right and Capello was a fool. I also had an issue with Rooney's strike partner Emile Heskey who would end his international career with sixty-two caps and a grand total of seven goals, an appalling return for a centre-forward. Especially when you consider in the same era and often playing on the same side at centre-back, John Terry was only one goal behind in his seventy-eight caps. Supporters of the muscular striker argued that he would bring others into the game, yet to have such an impotent strike rate and still get picked, I would actually expect him to bring players back from the dead. I was glad when after a painful goalless game with Algeria that he was replaced for England's final group game against Slovenia, although he did manage to avoid making any negative headlines as he left the pitch, unlike Rooney.

Rooney's Rage and the French Farce

After a second successive draw and a poor performance to boot, the fans that had paid exorbitant sums trekked the near 1,000 miles from Rustenburg to Cape Town, a long journey if you live in England, to let their feelings be known with a chorus of boos.

As England's number 10 walked off the pitch, instead of looking contrite and offering words of encouragement or an embarrassed apology, he stared deeply into the camera and decided criticising supporters was the order of the day. "Nice to see your home fans booing you. Loyal supporters." To me this was no surprise as he always looked ready to explode. He reminded me of the bloke down the pub who everybody was a little wary of, but you personally had no issues with, and for the last six months had been on nodding terms. Until one time, when you acknowledged his presence in the normal way, he would suddenly start screaming "What are you looking at?" while everybody else dived for cover. I was becoming more and more disillusioned with England, not the notion of supporting the country but the majority of the players filling the shirts. The last time I felt any real connection was in the 1990s.

This game was screened on ITV, so adverts were part of the programming and I have a feeling his outburst was not caught live but shown after an ad break. If that recollection is correct, I believe ITV are just as at fault as the player. England were playing poorly. The public were unhappy with them so why stoke the flames?

The England players had complained of boredom while being holed up for a couple of weeks at the out-of-the-way hotel in Rustenburg and maybe the base was a bit too isolated, but what was to be done after the shenanigans in Germany?

This was 2010, not the Stone Age; there would have been plenty of ways to keep themselves entertained, thanks to modern technologies. Or old ones, such as books.

Boxers at the highest level are often away from their families in isolated camps that last for eight or even twelve weeks and they cope. Sometimes they will do it two or three times a year. They understand for the ultimate rewards you must make the greatest sacrifice. It is not to fight angry; it is to ensure the fighter walks into the ring on fight night at their absolute peak.

The next day the players had a day off and were offered a chance to tour Robben Island where Nelson Mandela spent year after year in prison. Unfortunately, they declined to take up the invitation. Perhaps they should have gone. Not only would this have given them an insight into real boredom but maybe they would have taken some inspiration. During the 1995 Rugby World Cup, the South African team did visit and some of the players such as James Small were visibly moved to tears. A football side that did go during the World Cup were the Netherlands. Whether this had any bearing on those two teams still being alive on the last day of their respective tournaments we will never know. The simple fact was that they were and England would fall way short.

At least England's future record goal scorer did not decide to take industrial action. The French, who as a nation know more about going on strike than having great strikers, thought the World Cup with the eyes of the globe on them was the appropriate place for such action. After starting the tournament with a turgid 0–0 they were being held at half-time by Mexico, again with nothing recorded on the scoreboard. Clap-happy Domenech, who was somehow still in charge despite being derided by much of France, decided an ineffectual Nicolas Anelka needed to be replaced. This led to a blazing row between the manager and the player known as the 'Incredible Sulk'. The president of the French Football Federation suggested Anelka apologise. He refused and was sent home.

The next day's training brought things to a head. Captain Patrice Evra had a row with the fitness coach Robert Duverne and Domenech intervened.

Within moments, good old Patrice had flounced off to the team bus, quickly followed by his colleagues, where they sat with the curtain drawn like the old lady that disapproves of the young couple living in sin across the road. When they emerged, they had a letter for Domenech to read out outlining their support for their now absent colleague. The players knew the manager was leaving after the tournament and did not care about his feelings or opinions. As the row escalated, the French sent in their sports minister who made a plea so moving that some of the players were brought to tears and the mutiny on the bus was over. The team prepared to face South Africa in their last group game knowing they needed to win and hoping the other result in their group went their way. At half-time they were trailing by two goals and down to ten men. Yoann

Gourcoff had been sent off for an elbow that earned him a straight red. Bafana Bafana won the game but became the first hosts to go out at the group stage, losing out on goal difference to the Mexicans. Yet they had achieved something far more important. As rugby had before, sport had crossed the colour divide in the country and brought black and white together in support of the national side.

England faced Slovenia in the first and as it would turn out, only one of the nation's games that would cause any disruption to most people's working week. John Terry at the back must have felt like he was at some sort of speed dating conference as he found he had yet another partner at the heart of the defence, Matthew Upson. Slovenia found themselves unexpectedly at the top of the group and as all four teams could still progress or find themselves on a flight home, both games mattered. Defoe, who was belatedly in for Heskey, scored the winning goal to send England through in second place in the group of dearth, behind the Americans who beat Algeria.

Later that day, World Cup history was made. Brothers playing together at this level is common enough, on occasions even winning the trophy, such as Fritz and Ottmar Walter for Germany in 1954 and the Charlton boys of England in 1966.

Yet when Germany faced Ghana, sibling rivalry was on display for the first time at a finals. Jerome Boateng lined up for the Europeans, brother Kevin-Prince for the Africans. Both players were born in Berlin but Kevin, who had opted to play for the land of his father, was seen as a villain in Germany, not so much for this decision but because of a challenge in the FA Cup final that denied Die Mannschaft the services of their captain Michael Ballack in South Africa.

Although Germany came out on top, Ghana became the only one of the six African nations to make it through to the knockout stages.

During that World Cup I regularly hit my daily target early on, so I was often back to see the afternoon game and occasionally the lunchtime match. That made South Africa the World Cup during which I had watched the most matches for some time.

One day on which I did not achieve such success was the day Group F was decided. World champions Italy, who had yet to win a game, were facing Slovakia. I was listening on the car radio in between calls to the section's other game, as Paraguay played out a 0–0 draw with New Zealand, meaning a draw would see Italy through.

The radio station kept cutting to the more dramatic tie between the European sides and it would have been better if they had just stayed with it, as Italy, who had been trailing by two goals, halved the deficit going into the home straight. One more goal would be enough as they piled on the pressure, and one came in the eighty-ninth minute but it was scored in the Italian net. They still had time to pull one back but not two as they crashed out at the group stage meaning neither of the finalists from 2006 made it to the knockout rounds. Both finished behind New Zealand, who, thanks to three draws, were the only team to remain undefeated during the tournament.

Bad Decisions

On the first day of the knockout games Uruguay and Ghana won their ties to set up a quarter-final match, the winning goals scored by Luiz Suarez and Asamoah Gyan, men unaware that their names would be forever connected because of the upcoming game.

Next up were England versus Germany on a scorching hot Sunday afternoon when a decision by the referee would get one of the nations, plus a certain TalkSPORT commentator, extremely hot under the collar. Capello had made history by picking an unchanged side for the first time during his reign and England would make more before the day was out. I was watching at home with a few friends and once England had gone two down with just over half an hour played, thanks to strikes from the German's Polish-born strike pairing of Lukas Podolski and Klose, one of those in attendance, Gary, decided to take his little boy out for a push in the stroller and when he returned about thirty minutes later walked into a room in uproar.

England had already pulled one back when almost immediately Lampard hit a shot from outside the area that hit the underside of the bar and bounced down two or three feet over the line. Like Argentina in 1998 and while England celebrated, the opposition were still playing. The spin on the ball had sent it back into the field of play, the officials having missed it crossing the line. England fans have argued ever since that the momentum of the game would have changed and the result could, should or would have been completely different. On this occasion I disagree. The Three Lions had looked poor all tournament, including the first thirty-six minutes of the game, so having one minute of getting things right was not enough. Germany would have just regrouped and won the game anyway. Two second period goals gave Germany the game 4–1 and history England wanted to avoid, their record defeat at the finals. Later in the week I heard some highly entertaining radio commentary from that day. TalkSPORT's Mark Saggers completely lost control, raging, "Are you FIFA? Are you FIFA?" at anybody who happened to cross his path or had the slightest look of officialdom.

As my guests trooped home with emotions ranging from anger to desolation, myself and Gail settled down to watch our adopted team Mexico take on Maradona's Argentina. El Diez was back on the biggest stage of all as his country's manager, who had an embarrassment of attacking riches. He named six strikers in his squad. Although they could be suspect at the back, Maradona's philosophy was that his forward players could carry his team to glory and that day started with a front three of Gonzalo Higuaín, Carlos Tévez and the player who would draw so many comparisons to him, Lionel Messi.

On a bad day for the officials, Tévez put the South Americans one up with a header after being further offside than Lampard's shot was over the line. The Mexican appeals and the sense of injustice were further fuelled when the stadium's big screen showed a replay of the incident, something it was not supposed to do.

Argentina were too good a team against whom to concede a goal start and they progressed 3–1.

Blatter apologised to the English and the Mexican football associations and of course put all the blame on the match officials, whilst blatantly ignoring his own opposition to goal-line technology. Had it been in place Lampard would have been credited with a goal. While personally not a fan of VAR, the close calls are still too subjective, I have always been in favour of goal-line technology. The ball is over the line, or it is not. No debate. Just yes or no, in or out. Thankfully that day did lead to the introduction of goal-line technology at the 2014 finals.

By the time the first knockout stage was complete, the quarter-finals were made up of three ties that pitched South American sides against

European ones, the only outlier being Ghana against Uruguay. Four years earlier all the semi-finalists had been from Europe. Was this going to be a clean sweep for the South Americans? Whoever won, the viewing public was hoping that the players would get a better grip on the rogue ball, as up to that stage, Opta statistics confirmed there had been more misplaced passes than at any of the previous four World Cups.

In the very first quarter-final the prospect of the four South American teams contesting the semi-finals disappeared. A Brazilian team who, a wonderful Maicon goal against North Korea apart, failed to spark the imagination like in so many previous incarnations, went down 2–1 to the Dutch. The Netherlands had won their fifth game on the bounce.

The match that followed would turn out be the most memorable of the whole month as the planet's footballing eyes were focused on Africa.

Ghana had become known as Ghana Ghana in a play on the nickname of the host nation. The last African country standing not only had the support of the continent but many neutrals around the globe.

When they walked out in their kit, one that resembled Melchester Rovers from the comic book *Roy of the Rovers*, not even the script writers that kept me entertained as a child could have dreamt up the ending that lay ahead. Ghana took the lead in added time at the end of the first period and if they could keep from conceding after the break, would become the first African side to ever make the semi-finals. With the tournament's two strongest teams, Spain and Germany, on the other side of the draw, the final was also not out of the question.

In the second half Diego Forlan, who would go on to win the Golden Ball and was one of the few players that appeared to have conquered the Jabulani, scored with a wicked free-kick to set up a dramatic finale.

The game had found its way into extra time and then gone beyond the allotted thirty minutes when Ghana had one last chance. They swung a free-kick into the box and Luis Suárez blocked a shot on the line, then a header, but the second block was with his hand. He was not the only one on his team that was prepared to use this appendage. Left-back Jorge Fucile had dived to try and save it but missed, leaving Uruguay's fate quite literally in Suarez's hands. He received a straight red and penalty duties fell to Gyan who was the top scoring African player with three goals, two from the spot. If he could be successful once more from 12 yards out, Ghana the World Cup semi-finalists would be the message sent around the world. Instead, he hit the bar and while the ball was still in the air the referee blew for full-time. That is how close the Black Stars had come to making history. It was now down to a penalty shoot-out. With Uruguay one up in the final act, Gyan, in an extreme show of bravery, was the player who emerged from the Ghana ranks and scored with a penalty high into the net.

In the end the South Americans were the superior side from the spot, but Ghana had captured people's hearts and I have never felt so gutted for an international team that were not England.

While the world painted Suarez as a villain, I did not see him in that light. What he did was just a reaction that many other players, well, at least Fucile, would have done. It was not a dangerous tackle, a dive or something he tried to conceal from the referee. And after all he still had not reached the heights of his World Cup villainy. That was to come four years later.

What I did disagree with was the way he celebrated Gyan's penalty miss. I thought he could have shown a little more class at that point.

Germany booked their customary semi-final spot thanks to a 4–0 victory over Argentina (the third time they had scored four in South Africa) that showed a strong forward presence and the charisma of Maradona was not enough in the latter stages; they needed a decent defence and a semblance of tactics.

The ultimate place in the last four would belong to Spain or Paraguay and like most people, I was fairly convinced it would belong to the La Roja despite their opening game defeat to Switzerland.

The two sides swapped penalty misses before David Villa decided the tie with his fifth goal of the finals.

The Furious Final

It was the Dutch and the Spanish that made it through to the tournament's last game meaning that a squad containing seven Barcelona players, masters of tika-taka, a style of play that would not be affected by the poor aerodynamics of the ball, would face the Netherlands, a nation famed for their total football approach that they hoped would produce ultimate glory.

The football revolution that had led to Spain's distinctive style had its roots firmly established in the Netherlands, thanks to Rinus Michels and later Johan Cruyff. Both men were born in Amsterdam and played for and managed Ajax before landing in the Barcelona hot seat, where they imposed the style that is still evident at the Catalan club and was subsequently transferred to the national side with ease.

With these pedigrees, I was hoping for an entertaining final. As I watched with Gail, the first one we had watched together, what came next was a disappointment.

Spain had at the heart of their midfield the Barcelona duo of Xavi and Andres Iniesta, who had been swapping Man of the Match honours since the last group game. The key to success was stopping them. The tone was set in the fifteenth minute of a game that had more cards than many people receive for Christmas, when Robin van Persie collected the first of fourteen yellows shown. The match obliterated the highest previous final card count of six. Nine of these went to the Dutch and by the time the game finished, only Wesley Sneijder and Dirk Kuyt of their outfield players who started the game that night had not been cautioned.

Nigel de Jong was extremely lucky to only see yellow for a dreadful chest-high kick on Xabi Alonso. Referee Howard Webb has admitted if he had a better view, it would have been red and the Dutch would have faced over an hour with ten men. In the second half of a stop-start game Puyol was lucky not to receive a second yellow. With neither defence having been breached in normal time the game went into extra time where the prospect of a red card looked more likely than that of a goal.

In the hundred and ninth minute John Heitinga was booked for a second time and was off. Spain now did have a man advantage that should have been theirs much earlier.

With four minutes remaining the ball was at the feet of Iniesta, who was the calmest man in the stadium, and he scored the goal that Spain had craved for seventy-six years.

He would also get booked for his celebration as he removed his shirt to reveal a message that was a tribute to his friend and former Espanyol captain Dani Jarque, who had passed away during the previous August.

Although La Roja had played in their away strip of blue shirts, when they received the trophy they had changed into their more familiar red ones, embossed with a gold star that only eight teams have the right to, the symbol that says we have won the World Cup. Spain at last had beaten their quarter-final syndrome and could deservedly call themselves champions. Despite all the negative pre-tournament headlines, the trouble in South Africa remained mainly on the pitch.

BRAZIL 2014

At Last

It finally was going to happen. I was going to go to a World Cup and what better place than Brazil, the home of the 'jogo bonito'.

It somehow seemed fitting that a dream that started in Argentina with their ticker-tape-strewn pitches was coming to fruition next door, after the competition had travelled around the world to Europe, North America, Asia and Africa before coming back to South America.

Yet it so nearly did not happen.

The FIFA ticket website offered a choice of packages where you could either choose to follow a country with no idea where they would play or select a city with no idea of who would perform there.

England had qualified top of their group but not in any real style, drawing four out of their ten matches and were still too reliant on Gerrard and Lampard. They were now under the stewardship of Roy Hodgson who had beaten off local resident and fan favourite for the job, Harry Redknapp. At the time, while everybody was predicting Harry would get the job in the wake of Capello's resignation shortly before the 2012 Euros, I always felt Hodgson would be more of an FA-style pick and I was proved right. Would Harry have been a better choice? I do not know, but he was popular with the media as well as the public, which would have helped a great deal and it would have been a fun ride while it lasted.

With this in mind, and the vastness of the country, Gail and I decided a package based in one city was more to our liking, meaning we could get to know the area we were in. We had been to Brazil a few years earlier and spent a fortnight in Natal so wanted to see somewhere new. On that holiday we met several Brazilians who were on vacation from places such as Rio and São Paulo and they all recommended the north over the south to visit. Going with that advice, we could choose from Recife, Manaus or Fortaleza.

Although we did not know who was playing where at this stage, there was one anomaly. As the hosts, the location of Brazil's three group games was known: São Paulo, Fortaleza and Brasilia. This made the choice simple, it had to be Fortaleza, guaranteeing I would see Brazil on home soil during a World Cup. Also, maybe England would get a game in the city, possibly even against the hosts.

We applied for the tickets and were entered into a ballot and then waited. A couple of months later I opened an email telling us we had been successful. When I told Gail, she could not believe it and everybody else I mentioned it to told me how lucky I was. I think some of them thought I had won the tickets. I had to point out I was paying a considerable sum for them.

When the draw was made, as well as keeping my normal keen eye on England's group, for the first time I was watching for a particular city.

The package included four group games plus a round of sixteen match, so five ties in all.

England were drawn in a Group D containing three ex-champions, themselves, Uruguay and Italy plus Costa Rica. Conventional wisdom was that the country better known for its wildlife and jungles than its footballing prowess would lose all their games to their more illustrious opponents. Hence, it was an any-two-from-three situation. The opening game of this section was the first game we had tickets to, Uruguay against Costa Rica. Later that day England would face Italy in the heart of the Amazon in Manaus. If only the fixtures had been the other way round.

By now we had a problem. In early 2011 we had adopted a ten-year-old German Shepherd; well, in reality, we were supposed to have him for two weeks. His owner never returned, but that is another story.

My mum always looked after him if we were away. They got on brilliantly; too well, it was a bit of a battle to get him back.

How would this affect my World Cup dream? It's a tale only dog lovers will understand.

For a long time, Jerry, or JJ as he became known, had been well and was unrecognisable from the downtrodden old boy that had turned up on our doorstep. Yet as he got older his hips started to go, common for the breed.

We bought him a doggy wheelchair, something I thought I would never do, but he was still so full of life and his only problem was his legs. Once it arrived, we took him for his first walk with it. He took to it immediately; in fact, too well, according to the manufacturers.

Once strapped in, JJ's desire to run saw the brackets begin to come loose. When we spoke to the distributor and explained the problem she rather haughtily replied, "Running, he's not supposed to be running in it!" Once it had become clear that she was only interested in the money these contraptions put in her pocket rather than being a dog lover, I turned to Gary who is far more practical than I. He soon came up with a solution that meant JJ could carry on in his normal fashion.

This new addition to his walking routine meant my mum could not look after him anymore as it was simply too much for her. We had curtailed all our travelling and were now looking ahead, wondering what we would do with him while we were in Brazil and whether we should leave him at all. The prospect that he might pass away while we were gone was a terrible one, especially with the way he had previously been abandoned.

We decided not to book any hotels or flights yet and just play it by ear.

In February he took a turn for the worse and passed away on Valentine's weekend, yet not before he had polished off a family-sized box of his favourite treat, shortbread.

It felt like he knew his dad wanted to go to the World Cup and if he hung on, I would not be able to, so he just decided it was time to go.

I was devastated; we both were. We had not been away for ages and needed a break and booked a couple of weeks in Mexico, where we put a deposit down on a house. When we came back and told our families it felt like that scene in *An American Werewolf in London* when the guys walk into the pub. They made every argument under the sun that what we had done was wrong, sometimes using logic and other times just saying things not even Richard Nixon could have thought up.

All the while, we had been keeping an eye on hotel prices and flights to Brazil that seemed to be going up on an hourly basis.

Then we struck lucky: Gail found a hotel that had not previously been available and now all she had to do was get time off work. As we had recently been away, she thought that her bosses might be a little awkward, but fate smiled on us. The director of her department, who had the final say, had joined her company from Reading FC, where he was the commercial director. He understood what a big deal this was for a football fan. He agreed and we booked the hotel and flights.

We would miss our first game. It was Gail's mum Barbara's eightieth birthday in June and she wanted to throw her a party, even though her mum never enjoyed those type of events. No matter how much I reminded Gail of this, she was adamant that she would want this one.

In the build-up to the tournament, England played Ecuador in a friendly that of course brought about an injury. A twenty-year-old Alex Oxlade-Chamberlain was having a fantastic game and looked like a player who could make the difference when it mattered. With the game past the hour mark and heavy tackles flying in, the obvious thing was to replace him, unless of course you were the England manager. Hodgson, who had picked the Ox in his very first game, paid for his folly when a few minutes later a challenge put the Arsenal youngster out of contention for the first couple of games at least. Even more baffling was the choice of opponents for the final warm-up game, Honduras. Anybody who had seen them play knew their style. It reminded me of some of the rougher pubs I had worked and the game predictably saw a host of cards, including a red for the Hondurans, and even Adam Lallana, who rarely had his name taken, made himself known to the referee that day.

Yet again when I saw the England squad, I was disappointed. The blend was not right and there were too many youngsters at the expense of experienced players like Ashley Cole and Michael Carrick. I was glad that I had not chosen to follow England, as once again, pessimism set in.

As the double header of Barbara's eightieth and the World Cup approached, it became clear she really did not want a party, instead just a family dinner on the day.

While that was being organised, I invited some friends round to watch the opening match between Brazil and Croatia on Thursday June 12. The day before the game, when I asked Gail what time we were expected at her mum's that night, she said that her birthday was on the 12th. I am still convinced that she told me it was the 11th. Well, that's my version of events and I am sticking to it. This scheduling conflict caused a problem. I dug my heels in and explained that I had never missed an opening game of the World Cup and as I was already missing the first game of our package, was not going to start now. As I have since discovered in writing this book, I had not seen every opening game, but believed I had.

The night when Brazil faced Croatia, a somewhat frosty-faced Gail went to her mum's birthday dinner while Steve, Gary and my friend from primary school Chris came round to watch a scintillating opening encounter which only took twelve minutes to make history. Brazil's Marcelo scored an own goal, the first time the opening goal of a tournament had been scored in such a manner.

Neymar, who was carrying the hopes of two hundred million people on his young shoulders, equalised and then in the second half put the Selecao in front from the spot after Fred went down easier than Bambi wearing ice-skates.

We had all chucked £2 into a kitty and picked a score; I had gone with 2–1 Brazil and had just stood up to collect the money when somehow Oscar's injury time shot made it past the Croat keeper to make it 3–1. I passed my 'winnings' over to Chris who had the correct score.

As well as the player who had the same name as one of your uncles, the Brazil squad contained Bernard, Jo, Victor and Oscar instead of the romantic names of yesteryear such as Rivellino, Ronaldinho, Pele, Garrincha and Zico. Even though they did not sound like the storied players of the past, the country expected, no, demanded, that they perform like them. Would this fairly inexperienced squad be able to cope? Only one of the outfield players who started their first game had more than fifty caps. They had won the Confederations Cup the year before, the test event played in each host country, comfortably beating world champions Spain 3–0 in the final to ramp up the pressure just a little more. They had also won the two previous versions in Germany and South Africa; however, in both countries just twelve months later, they would wave goodbye to their dreams at the quarter-final stages. There was no guarantee of success.

Before we left, I saw a repeat of the 2010 final in which Spain took the lead before Robin van Persie equalised with a sublime header, as the Dutch beat the all-conquering Spaniards by an implausible score of 5–1 in an excellent game. I had believed for a while, although he was one of the heroes of South Africa, that Iker Casillas should have been replaced in the Spanish goal by David De Gea and this game just confirmed it.

Suddenly after two World Cups which had featured a lot of poor games, the tide was turning. It was as if the players were as inspired as I was by the prospect of being in Brazil.

Two in Brazil

We left London on Saturday June 14 and flew to São Paulo before taking an internal flight to Fortaleza.

The Saturday night while we were in the air, England were due to face Italy, and I had heard rumours that some airlines could show live games. I had hoped this to be true but did not expect it to be. I was not disappointed, it wasn't.

We travelled with Portuguese national carrier TAP Air for the first leg, a company that put all the airlines that carry British holidaymakers to shame with their entertainment package. They had something like a hundred films available, ranging from 1950s classics to modern offerings at no extra charge.

Once we landed at São Paulo, chaos kicked in. People were everywhere, making Heathrow look like a provincial airport. We were guided in the vague direction of where to go and walked past piles of what appeared to be abandoned suitcases. This did not bode well for the onward journey of our luggage.

We were a little disoriented and found a kindly airport employee who took us to where we had to line up for the next leg of our journey. He explained to the people already waiting what was going on as he inserted us near the front of the queue, which everybody accepted apart from a Colombian couple quite a long way back who started shouting at us. The airport employee walked down the line and explained the situation. This appeared to appease them for a few minutes before the man decided he needed to go all macho and shout some more. By then we had moved through to the next area and I had made a mental note to support whoever played Colombia.

We arrived at our hotel in the evening, shattered, but delighted to be there, and much to Gail's delight, with all our luggage.

I attempted to place our valuables in the safe and realised that the key I had been given was the wrong one. Half asleep, I returned to reception who apologised and gave me a massive bunch of keys, telling me one would work. Feeling like a warder from the television programme *Prisoner: Cell Block H*, I made my way back to our room and eventually cracked the code.

In the morning I was awoken by Gail jangling the keys wanting to know what I had been up to, as she was asleep by the time I had returned from my hunting expedition. I explained that the front desk had given me the keys to all the room safes and told me to return them in the morning. Welcome to Brazil!

On the first day the hotel was quiet, and we spent it exploring our base that was situated on a hilltop overlooking Fortaleza itself. It was decent enough and had a nice pool with absolutely stunning views, but on closer inspection you could tell it had been so much more. We found an old disused pool and communal area that would have been breathtaking in its day and reasoned why it had suddenly become available to book online. Somebody had seen an opportunity, taken part of the hotel and made it ready for the finals. It was perfect for our needs.

We took in one game at the hotel bar. Portugal were carrying my money this time around. I had reasoned they were playing in a country with a shared language and although they had to come through the play-offs, they did have Cristiano Ronaldo who had scored a hat-trick to get them to Brazil in the first place.

It was not long before I realised that my money was down the drain, as in their very first game, Portugal had a player sent off and lost 4–0 to Germany. They were clearly not going to emulate their Iberian neighbours from four years ago.

The next day everything changed. When we entered the restaurant for breakfast we were met by an explosion of sound, colour and joyous chaos. The opposing fans were in town.

The team that we would see play Brazil in their own backyard were Mexico and with the restaurant suddenly being so busy we had to share a table and got talking with our dining companions. Virtually all of those that were following El Tri had made their homes in the States and spoke English. While we chatted, we explained that we had bought a house in Playa del Carmen which most of them had visited. They told us we were going to live in paradise.

The following day when we went back to the room to get changed, we had a dilemma. I owned one Mexican team shirt and one Brazilian. We tossed a coin and I ended up in green, Gail in yellow. We made our way to reception where we had agreed to meet some of the Mexican fans who had arranged a minibus to take us to the official FIFA coach, which would then take us right to the stadium. Or so we believed.

We piled on with everybody in green except for one lady; to anybody passing it must have looked like the kidnapping of a lone Brazilian fan. On the way they offered to teach us some Mexican football chants and while I was trying to learn the words, for some reason Gail started humming the tune, which just about made it impossible as I really did not speak much Spanish at this point. So, he changed tack and said when the Brazilian goalie had the ball, we should wave our hands and shout 'Puto', believing that was an easy enough instruction for us to follow. So he thought.

Once we arrived at the official pick-up point, we were separated onto a different coach. On the new bus journey we saw Brazil shirts for sale on every street corner, all of them emblazoned with only one name and number, Neymar and 10. The pressure on the country's star player was going to be off the scale. The other thing we noticed was how many businesses had shut for the day; it seemed the whole country was going to be tuning in. When we arrived at the drop-off point, we immediately wondered why we had so as early as we did, before realising we then had a route march to the stadium in scorching heat. The kick-off time for all our games was 2:00 p.m.

This really added to the atmosphere. We walked to the stadium down a roped-off road lined either side by Brazilians who I guessed lived in the immediate area that appeared to be cordoned off near the stadium. As we headed to the Castelao Stadium some of the locals called out to try and sell us food and drinks, while others just wanted to shake our hands. It was as if this gave them a bigger connection to the game.

It was a wonderful carnival atmosphere and we stopped for photos with fans of both teams. Outside the stadium, while we were soaking in the atmosphere, we were approached by a local radio station who asked us in English if they could interview us. Of course, we replied yes and were instantly on air, as they began to question how it was for us, with one being Brazilian and the other Mexican and how had we met. They were a little taken aback when I explained we were both English and had met outside Marks and Spencer in Bournemouth.

Once in the stadium we bought some drinks which came in Coca-Cola and Brahma, a Brazilian beer, branded cups with the venue, date and names of the two sides. I, like many others, took those cups home as mementos plus the ones from our other games.

The stadium was a sea of colour, the Brazilian fans in their familiar sun-drenched yellow and the Mexicans in a mix of green and their second strip of red that the players were wearing that day. The atmosphere ratcheted up another level as the two sets of supporters sang their respective national anthems. The moment I had wait so many years for had finally arrived, as Brazil kicked off against Mexico. If I could not be watching England take on the other team I had followed at every World Cup, Mexico, where I was going to make a new life, was the perfect substitute.

So many things to take in and enjoy, so many things to try and remember.

Within the first minute Neymar was fouled and rolled in comical fashion.

On the side-lines, the Mexican manager encouraged his team throughout the game like a chubby jack-in-the-box.

Ochoa the Mexican goalkeeper played a tremendous game including one first half save from Brazil's number 10 that looked near impossible.

The other player who impressed whilst on his feet was Neymar himself; seeing him live I realised just how much he did for his team.

We were seated next to a Brazilian couple and when the man said a simple phrase in Spanish, I understood and replied. The crowd had pockets of supporters for each team all mixed together, but there was absolutely no hint of trouble. We soon realised the chant we had been taught was not only for when the Brazilian keeper had the ball but whenever they missed an opportunity or made a mistake, so we were soon joining in with the shout of 'Puto'. Well, I was. Gail had completely misheard what we had been told on the bus and was shouting 'Pluto', thinking we were calling the opposition some sort of dirty dog. If anybody had been watching her, I am sure their sense of bemusement would have been added to by the fact she was wearing a Brazilian shirt whilst abusing their players.

The game ended 0–0 but it was a tremendous contest, probably the best goalless one I have ever seen.

I have been to games at Wembley, Old Trafford, the Bernabéu and Signal Iduna Park, to name just a few, but the atmosphere that day trumped all of them put together.

When we left, we saw people holding signs asking for used tickets, but I decided I was going to keep ours as souvenirs and it was only once I got back to England that I realised what was going on. There is an online market for used tickets, so these people were collecting them to sell on.

As we walked back towards the coach, we spotted a guy walking his dog who he had dressed in a Brazil shirt and an old boy who noticed us holding hands waved his finger at Gail as if to tell her she should not be fraternising with the enemy.

I had seen my first game at the World Cup and if that had been the only game, I would have been content, but there was more to come.

That night we decided to eat out and found many restaurants just starting to reopen after the game, before returning to the hotel tired and full and satisfied. On the way to our room, we bumped into some Mexicans that we had not travelled to the game with and asked them exactly what 'Puto' meant. They explained it could mean many things, but in this case the nearest English word was faggot, so definitely nothing Disneyesque about it.

FIFA requested the Mexican fans not use this word anymore yet were completely ignored.

They do not see what they are doing as offensive, it is just a bit of fun to add to the atmosphere. Here language is something to be played with, words embraced rather than feared. For example, my barber is nicknamed *pato* (duck) because he walks a bit like one. Who gave him this rather unflattering nickname? His parents.

Fan Park

The next morning at breakfast two American guys who were brothers joined us. Russ lived in New York, the other had married a Hispanic woman and now resided in the Dominican Republic. I cannot recall his name so I will call him Dave.

As we chatted, I mentioned how good the previous day's match had been and mentioned that I hoped we would see some goals next time.

Now I have a very clear English accent but have found, bizarrely, that Americans who are listening in their first language often find it a lot harder to understand me than Mexicans in a second. This was one of those occasions.

Russ said, "Yes, it would be great to see some girls" and did I know a good bar. I had to point out that I was talking about goals not girls and all of this took place in front of my girlfriend.

Despite this slightly awkward start we got on well and arranged to go to the Fortaleza fan park the next day to watch the England versus Uruguay tie, a game both teams were desperate to get something from after losing their opener. Italy had beaten England 2–1 while we were in the air.

The atmosphere was again fantastic with fans from all around the world in attendance and plenty of entertainment in addition to the game. England decided to torture their supporters by managing to concede a winner with only five minutes left, yet this time the loss somehow felt worse in front of witnesses from across the globe.

Suarez had scored both of Uruguay's goals and each time he was given so much space you would have thought it was 2020 and the English defence was strictly adhering to the COVID-19 social distancing rules.

A second 2–1 defeat left the Three Lions on the brink of elimination, which was confirmed the next day when Costa Rica beat Italy.

At least Rooney had broken his World Cup scoring drought, his only ever goal at the finals, a woeful return for a player of his natural ability.

Germany-Ghana

The second game we had tickets for was Germany and Ghana on the Saturday, featuring the Boateng boys facing each other once again.

By now, most of the Mexicans had left our hotel and on the Friday morning when we went to breakfast, we were greeted by a sea of blonde hair. The German fans had arrived. The atmosphere in the room was markedly different; where you would have struggled to hear a mariachi band when the Mexicans were in town, now the sound was polite gentile conversation. The other change was poolside.

The Mexicans did not sunbathe, so we had the pool area virtually to ourselves, yet when we made our way to the pool this time, we were lucky to claim the last two sunbeds. This may seem like a stereotype, but it was true. At least the Germans were actually using them. The Brits can be just as guilty. On our previous trip to Brazil we stayed in a hotel that was mainly being occupied by my countrymen and if you were not up before dawn you struggled for a sunbed, many of which would not be troubled by human flesh until around 11:00 a.m.

The day of the game, we shared a taxi with our American buddies to the coach pick-up point. As Dave spoke Spanish—while the Brazilians speak Portuguese many can understand Spanish, yet all the Mexicans told us they could not follow Portuguese—we let him deal with the driver. As he took his seat in the front of the cab, he confidently told us that he had negotiated a good, fixed price deal, so good that the driver would put the metre on to show the saving we were making. Sure enough, it would have been a few reals more.

Once at the coach stop, I noticed many people with German flags painted on their faces who distinctly did not look as if they were from Germanic stock. They were not; lots of Latin people were supporting them, which all the neutral Europeans found odd, as we were all rooting for the African underdogs.

Before the game, we were taking to a couple of German guys who asked me if I knew anything about the 'Puto' cry and with the 4–1 from South Africa still in my mind the devil got the better of me.

I explained that it was a word of encouragement and that every time the German keeper took a goal kick, they should shout it as loudly as they could.

Once seated and with them being a few rows in front of us, I noticed that they took my advice to heart, even turning round a couple of times to give me the thumbs up.

We found ourselves in a similar part of the stadium but in a different row, seated next to the same Brazilian couple. The gentleman heard us talking in English and asked where we were from. I explained that we were from England and he told me he thought I was Mexican. The power of a shirt.

The game, what a game, the best live one I have attended.

After a goalless first half, we were treated to a breathtaking second. Germany took the lead when Mario Gotze's header rather fortuitously hit his knee to give his side the lead. With everybody now expecting the Germans to increase it, the opposite materialised.

Within three minutes the scores were level, within twelve, Gyan had put Ghana into the lead. As his right foot shot hit the back of the net, one of the African supporters several rows down from us celebrated so hard his popcorn flew out of its container, landing on those around him. Then something I had never seen happen in a stadium before occurred. The support changed; all the neutrals who had been cheering Germany on now flipped their allegiance and were urging on the Ghanaians. As I looked around me people were trying to rub the red, yellow and black from their faces.

Ghana kept pushing and could have easily gone two goals up before Germany introduced Miroslav Klose who equalised with his first touch, a goal that drew him level as the World Cup's all-time leading scorer with Ronaldo on fifteen.

Neither team sat back, they both pushed for a winner, one that would not come as both sides left with a point.

On the coach as we left the venue, we were accompanied by a load of Aussie guys, who were great fun and singing rugby songs. One of them inadvertently made me laugh when he asked if I had seen "Timmy's goal", referring to Tim Cahill's cracking strike against the Netherlands. I was amused because I was imagining a country that we see as macho worshipping a guy called Timmy? In England, only librarians are called Timmy.

Greece-Ivory Coast

We had more trips to the fan park. The first to watch the USA play Portugal. Feeling torn, on the surface I was supporting the USA as our new American buddies had so raucously cheered on England on our previous visit, but I needed Portugal to come through for my bet. A 2–2 draw effectively put Portugal out, but the Americans could still be overhauled by the Ghanaians, especially if they played like they did against Germany.

Then we got to experience watching Brazil with their fans away from the stadium.

Their last group game saw them pitted against Cameroon and with nothing guaranteed another fantastic atmosphere was created.

The location of the FIFA Fan Fest was on the beach and although some people choose to stand, you could always find somewhere to sit and have a great view of the massive screen.

Neymar scored twice in the first half and both times, an old lady, who must have been closing in on seventy, ran up to the screen and blew kisses for a couple of minutes towards her hero on the giant television.

At the same time a young Brazilian lad wearing the tightest of budgie smugglers jumped up and Dave, in a deadpan manner, observed, "Everybody in Brazil has an ass."

We visited the onsite shop and although I vowed not to be taken in by the overpriced merchandise, when I saw models of the grounds, I wanted one of the Fortaleza Stadium. The problem was that everybody else in town had the same idea and they were sold out, with no more stock expected. Instead, I settled for a colourful t-shirt.

I had already been given a small cuddly toy of the mascot Fuleco, a three-banded armadillo. When Gail's stepmum gave it to me, I may have seemed a little ungrateful. I was a forty-seven-year-old man, what did I want with a cuddly toy? The experience at the finals changed all of that; he still sits on my desk to this very day.

Our third game was the pivotal battle between Greece and the Ivory Coast.

That morning, England were playing Costa Rica in what was for them a dead rubber but if Los Ticos could get a result, they could top the group. As a poor game edged towards a 0–0 finish, I switched over to the Uruguay v Italy clash that had something riding on it for both teams. Virtually straight away I saw Italian centre-half Giorgio Chiellini, whose face looks like it was made from the rock that Mount Rushmore was chiselled, pulling down his shirt and showing the referee his shoulder in some bizarre Alan-Partridge-meets-international-football moment. Suarez was on the floor holding his rather sizeable gnashers; he had bitten his marker. Sadly, this was not new behaviour for the striker, he had previously bitten opponents when he was playing for Liverpool and Ajax. He got away with it on the day but was subsequently banned for nine internationals. Diego Godin had grabbed a late winner with the Italians still up in arms. This meant La Celeste went through as runners-up to shock group top dogs Costa Rica. Italy's stay in Brazil was curtailed.

For the two previous games our hotel had been invaded by supporters of Mexico and Germany; the Greek army was a little smaller. In fact, it consisted of just one rather overweight guy.

We arranged to share a taxi with him to the coach pick-up point. When we came down to meet him, he had disappeared faster than the Greek economy, so we found ourselves on our own. By now our American buddies had gone back stateside so I hopped in the front. I noticed the tariff the driver was using was B, the same one that had been used on every other journey that Dave had so confidently informed us was more than the fixed price deals he was getting.

On the windows in the front of the cabs two tariffs were displayed and it turned out during the day we should have been charged tariff A which was significantly cheaper.

I pointed this out to our driver, and he adjusted the rate. After some fake apology, we had by far the cheapest ride into town yet.

It turned out that virtually all the taxi drivers coming to our hotel, which was a good few miles out, were in on it. The lesson I learnt was not to trust a Brazilian taxi driver or an American to read the details.

At the game it was clear one player above all others was the star attraction. With the score at 1–1 and with seventy-seven minutes on the clock, Didier Drogba of the Ivory Coast was substituted to a thunderous round of applause from the whole ground.

With Colombia leading Japan, a draw would be enough for the Africans to progress.

In the third minute of injury time Georgios Samaras kicked the turf and went down inside the area and the referee erroneously awarded a penalty, which the Greek striker converted to send his side through. Another country's World Cup dream shattered unfairly. With Costa Rica lying in wait, the Ivory Coast would have fancied their chances of at least emulating Ghana from four years earlier and making the last eight.

That night we ate out, as we had done on several occasions—some planned, others not, as randomly and with no warning some evenings the hotel restaurant did not open.

Not for the first time, we went to a Rodizio, a meat eater's heaven, especially in a country famed for their steaks.

These are set price restaurants that have huge buffets with a tempting selection of food such as pastas, salads, cold meats and cheeses but the star attraction is served at your table.

Your waiter comes around with a skewer of meat, for example, beef, and he will carve you as much or as little as you want. Then, just as you are tucking in, his buddy will appear with some chicken and go through the same routine. Then another arrives, maybe with lamb or sausage, and this goes on all night until you finally surrender. The only weapon you are given to defend yourself is a piece of wood or card that has red on one side, green the other, and when you need a break or can cram in no more, you opt to show the red side.

When we arrived back at our hotel, we started discussing the fifth game of our package which pitched Netherlands against Mexico. By coincidence, the Mexicans are obsessed with playing a fifth game at the finals, or as it is known here, 'el quinto partido'.

This was the sixth World Cup in a row that they had reached the knockout stage. Yet in every tournament since 1994 their journey had ended in the round of sixteen. They were desperate to get to the quarter-finals and play that fabled fifth game.

Unfortunately, we had booked only eleven nights in Brazil; this, along with our trip to Mexico, had used up virtually all of Gail's holiday allocation for the year. Somebody who had in reality gone so I could realise my dream had been taken by the experience so much and was now asking if we could change our flights and stay on.

Changing the flights would have been the easy bit, but before we left, I had returned the tickets for the two games that fell outside of our stay. The FIFA website had said that if the tickets were re-sold we would get some money back. We never did.

Knockout and Knocked Out

The only benefit of this was that we would arrive back home in time for the start of the knockout games.

With the matches played at 5:00 p.m. and 9:00 p.m. it was easy to watch them. I consumed each and every one, including the third-place play-off, always accompanied by Gail.

Although maybe a little influenced by the fact that just a few days earlier we were amid the action, I recall most of the games providing entertaining fare.

Of course, the game we looked on at with the most envious eyes saw Mexico lining up against the Netherlands, a game that made history.

A rule had been introduced stating that if the temperature exceeded 32 degrees, cooling breaks would be taken to allow the players to take on liquids and rehydrate and this was the first match for which it was implemented. Another innovation at these finals was the introduction of a vanishing spray. Once the referees had given a free-kick and paced out the 10 yards where the offending team could stand, they would draw a line with the water-based spray and mark where the dead ball would be played from. It would then rapidly disappear leaving no unsightly marks on the playing surface.

It is a welcomed idea that should not be needed but is, due to the constant attempts of most teams in these situations to gain a few centimetres.

The Mexicans had taken the lead soon after the break thanks to a fantastic goal from Giovanni Dos Santos, a strike the Mexican fans would call a *golazo*. With the full-time whistle approaching they sat back for too much. Having nobody in a forward position meant that every time they cleared their lines the ball would come straight back and with two minutes left the inevitable equaliser came.

Then into injury time the day got worse for the team in green.

Arjen Robben deceived the referee into awarding him a penalty which Klass-Jan Huntelaar put away and Mexico had fallen at the all-too-familiar hurdle.

Of the eight games in that round, five went to extra time but only two all the way to shoot-outs. Two of those matches decided in the additional thirty minutes saw three goals scored; nobody was settling for penalties. Additionally, in five of those ties, goalkeepers took home the Man of the Match trophy, a sure sign that there had been plenty of goalmouth action.

In the quarter-finals, two games had particularly decisive moments. With Brazil leading my new nemesis Colombia 2–1 and the final whistle less than five minutes away, Neymar received a knee in the back that not only put him out of the tournament but shook the Brazilian side and nation to its core. Although they did manage to hold on to qualify for the semi-finals.

In the last quarter-final Costa Rica played out a game with the Netherlands that remained goalless after extra time. At the last possible moment Dutch coach Louis van Gaal made a bold move when he substituted his first-choice keeper Jasper Cillessen with Tim Krul. I saw this as a clever psychological ploy. Even if the two keepers were on a par in stopping spot-kicks, the opposition are going to think the custodian coming on is the better one. And if he can save one early, as he did with Costa Rica's second attempt, extra doubts would creep into the minds of those facing him. The plan worked. Netherlands went through.

The semi-finals were made up of familiar names. Firstly, the hosts would battle Germany then Argentina would lock horns with the Dutch.

The Brazil-Germany semi-final is never to be forgotten, yet all of Brazil wishes it could be. Brazil were without their injured talisman plus skipper Thiago Silva who was banned due to collecting two yellow cards. David Luiz would be wearing the armband. Although I expected Germany to win quite easily, maybe even by three or four goals, I was still shocked by what followed. We of course were rooting for the country that had made us so welcome, taxi drivers apart—although the first sign of trouble for me came when I saw the Brazilians singing their national anthem. The skipper for the day was holding a Neymar shirt high in the air whist belting out the words. Too much energy and too much emotion was being expended on an absent player.

Then the most unbelievable thing transpired. Brazil, who had not lost a competitive game on home soil since 1975, found themselves trailing 5–0 inside thirty minutes. To give that some context, when Australia beat American Samoa 31–0, the Aussies had scored eleven at the same point in time, over twice as many. Yet this was against the most successful country and team in World Cup history. With such a shocking score-line, the fact that Klose scored the second goal of the day to take him out on his own as the World Cup's all-time leading marksmen seems to have been forgotten outside of Germany.

Once it got to four Gail kept saying that the Germans should stop now, that was enough. They had no consideration for her feelings and ran out 7–1 winners, to leave the country that adores football more than any other wishing the game had never been played. At the end Gail was almost in tears, she had so wanted them to take the trophy.

David Luiz gave an interview where he was battling back tears that summed up how the country felt. Although we had wished we were still in Brazil we were glad we had left before this game. We did not want to witness their sad humiliation up close.

Hardly surprisingly considering the drama that unfolded, my memory of Argentina overcoming Netherlands in the other semi-final on penalties is minimal.

In the final Germany overcame Argentina in a game that did not live up to those that had come before it, thanks to a Mario Gotze effort in extra time. The German side had played some excellent football over the last month and were worthy winners. Our World Cup adventure was over; well, nearly.

On the Monday after, Gail came home with an unexpected small windfall. She had entered a sweepstake at work and had drawn Brazil as the team that would concede the most goals, something we never expected to pay out yet it was a winner even before the 3–0 defeat in the bronze medal match. They had unbelievably beaten Australia and Cameroon, who finished thirtieth and thirty-second, to this unwanted milestone.

It had taken thirty-six years, the death of my beloved dog and missed opportunities but I can finally say that I was there and in probably the best country to be so. If you have the slightest inkling that you want to go to a finals, in the words of a company that had produced some entertaining football-based adverts, "Just Do It."

EPILOGUE

2014 was a fantastic World Cup to attend, with plenty of attacking football and along with France 1998 had the most goals of any thirty-two-team finals. Even though this was an antidote to the defensive football that had dominated the last couple of tournaments, England was once again a disappointment.

Enter Gareth Southgate, who, after taking up the manager's job after a newspaper made allegations of malpractice against previous incumbent Sam Allardyce, has restored hope.

He led England to the semi-finals of the 2018 World Cup and the final of the delayed 2020 European Championship, where of course they lost on penalties.

Yes, they had relatively easy runs in the knockout stages both times; the difference was that they actually achieved those runs at glory. The fact that England's three group games were poor at the Euros has already been consigned to the dustbin of forgotten memories, people instead remembering the excitement of a foray deep into the tournament. We watched the semi-final defeat from Russia in a bar in Mexico with a group of ex-pats and at the final whistle, with no prompting, we all stood and burst into applause.

It helps that the media likes Southgate, but the other huge plus is the players. This new group of youngsters, although still paid megabucks, somehow have made a connection with the fans that the golden generation did not.

When we were in Brazil many of the Mexican fans had been to two, three or even four of the previous tournaments. When I asked about going to Russia, it was about a 50/50 split of those intending to go and those who would not. As for Qatar, no-one was planning to attend. Along with not wanting to support that sham and believing it is not the right place to host the tournament anyway, I have no intention of spending my money to be part of it in person.

So I will just have to enjoy the spectacle as I did my very first tournament in 1978, on television, but with more in-depth coverage and my own bigger TV! For the first time since the 1990s, I actually like the England team and maybe, just maybe, I will see the land of my birth lift the World Cup one day. Please.

October 2022

ABOUT THE AUTHOR

Michael Renouf grew up in a small Wiltshire village in the UK. He was five years old when he realised there was a beautiful game beyond playing with matchbox cars and now in his 50s, not much has changed.

In 2015 he relocated to Mexico and began writing professionally, penning film reviews and sports features for magazines and websites around the world. Although he has left the country for sunnier climes he still supports England but thanks to their performances at previous tournaments now fervently hopes rather than believes, as he did for many years, that he will witness them lift the World Cup one day.

He lives with his long-term partner Gail, who doesn't support his team or totally get the offside rule, and lovable rescue dog Princesa, who has never chased a ball in her life.

Other really good football books from Fair Play Publishing

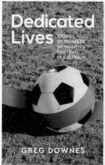

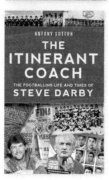

Football fiction from Popcorn Press
Anna Black
The End of the Game
Game
The Gaffer

Books about Life from Pepper Press
When A Soulmate Says No
Manjits and the Tandoor of Secrets